How to Retire Early

Your Unconventional Guide to Achieving Freedom Sooner Than You Ever Thought Was Possible

Andrew Holloway

© **Copyright 2019 - All rights reserved.**

The content contained within this book may not be reproduced, duplicated or transmitted without direct written permission from the author or the publisher.

Under no circumstances will any blame or legal responsibility be held against the publisher, or author, for any damages, reparation, or monetary loss due to the information contained within this book. Either directly or indirectly.

Legal Notice:

This book is copyright protected. This book is only for personal use. You cannot amend, distribute, sell, use, quote or paraphrase any part, or the content within this book, without the consent of the author or publisher.

Disclaimer Notice:

Please note the information contained within this document is for educational and entertainment purposes only. All effort has been executed to present accurate, up to date, and reliable, complete information. No warranties of any kind are declared or implied. Readers acknowledge that the author is not engaging in the rendering of legal, financial, medical or professional advice. The content within this book has been derived from various sources. Please consult a licensed professional before attempting any techniques outlined in this book.

By reading this document, the reader agrees that under no circumstances are is the author responsible for any losses, direct or indirect, which are incurred as a result of the use of information contained within this document, including, but not limited to, —errors, omissions, or inaccuracies.

Table of Contents

Chapter 1: Figuring Out How Much Money You Need to Retire..6

Chapter 2: The Correct Retirement Mindset You Need to Have to See Success...................................10

Chapter 3: Why You Should Increase Your Income to Retire Early...31

Chapter 4: What You Need to Know About 401(k)'s and IRA Accounts..44

Chapter 5: How to Save More Money to Make Early Retirement a Reality..55

Chapter 6: How to Get Out of Debt Efficiently and Effectively..79

Chapter 7: Tips to Help Improve Your Credit Score..86

Introduction:

I want to get straight to the point here—this book will not give you the same standard financial advice that you're used to hearing. And why should it? The simple fact of the matter is that most Americans are not in good financial situations.

It's estimated that 78% of Americans live paycheck to paycheck (1). Another survey found that nearly 42% of Americans have less than $10,000 saved for retirement (2). Clearly, something isn't working here.

Therefore, how could this book be the same? Giving you the same old advice that you've heard your whole life—go to school, get a job, work hard for 40 years, and then happily retire isn't working for people.

There are a lot of Americans out there who're working hard every day, yet their financial situation isn't getting any better. If you want to be able to retire early, then you must be different.

If you want to live a stress-free retirement where you're not worried about money or if you can travel or not, then this book is for you. In this book, you're going to have the step-by-step game plan you need to be able to retire early and comfortably.

Most people ignore their finances because they don't want to face the harsh financial situation that they currently find themselves in. You must be different than that though.

If right now you're not in the best spot when it comes to money, then accept that fact so you can improve it. It's not as if it's your fault.

No one teaches us anything about money when we're growing up. We don't learn much about money when we're in school. Therefore, the people we probably learned about money from were our parents.

And of course, depending on what you're parents financial lives were like, that advice could have been good or bad. Regardless of what you've learned in the past or what retirement situation you currently find yourself in, this book will help you to be able to turn things around.

I'm not going to lie to you and say that retiring early will be a walk in the park because it certainly won't be. However, if you stay focused and diligent with the advice found in this book, then you'll be able to do what most can't and that is to retire comfortably and early.

Also before we get into the nitty gritty of the book please consider leaving a review if you enjoy it. Even just a few words will help other people know if the book is right for them. Many thanks in advance!

Chapter 1: Figuring Out How Much Money You Need to Retire

One of the first steps that you must take if you want to retire early is to take the time and figure out how much it is that you need in order to retire. Most people never think about this.

They don't think about when they want to retire or how much it is that they'll need in order to retire. Without knowing this information, then you're really just hoping for the best.

You'll more than likely have to keep on working later than you want to or you'll have to live on less money than you'd like to. That can certainly cause stress no doubt.

Therefore the best thing that you can do is think about what kind of retirement you'd like to have. Set a goal for what age it is that you'd like to retire by.

Then think about what kind of retirement you'd like to have. Do you want to live mostly a simple retirement where you can live cheaply so that you don't have to work? Or do you want to travel the world?

These factors will affect how much money it is that you need so carefully think about it. After that, it's going to be time to get more into the nitty-gritty of how much money it is that you'll need to retire.

A popular rule of thumb is that you'll need between 70-85% of your preretirement income to live off of. This means that if your current annual income is $50,000 per year, then you'll need to have enough money stored away to be able to live off of between $35,000-$42,500 per year.

Of course, this rule may or may not be that accurate for you depending on what your goals are. For example, you might make $50,000 per year, but you might only be living on $25,000 per year.

In this case, you're already living on far less than 70-85% of your income and it's reasonable to think you could continue living on that amount once you retire. However, this is assuming that you're going to live a similar lifestyle to what you are right now after you retire.

If you're saving a lot of money right now to retire early, but you want to travel more once you retire, then you're going to need to have more money per year to live on.

Another popular rule for retirement is something known as the 4% rule. This basically states that you should withdrawal 4% of your nest egg per year during retirement.

For example, if you have 1.5 million saved for retirement, then you would live on 4% of that money per year, which in this case would equate to $60,000 per year. This rule is generally seen as safe by most because it can help to equate for inflation.

Assuming the annual market return is 7% and the average rate of inflation is 3% per year, then this could be a good way to calculate how much it is that you'll need to withdraw once you're retired.

Of course, this rule might only help you out if you're nearing retirement. If you're young and still a little ways away from retirement then this rule might not be of much use for you to be able to gauge how much it is that you'll need to retire comfortably.

If you're currently in this boat, then you might need to do something different to figure out how much it is you need to retire. The first place to start would be to determine how much it is that you want to live on per year when you retire.

Let's say for the sake of example that you determine you want to live off of $50,000 per year once you retire. Then you're going to take that number and multiply it by the number of years that you expect to be retired.

Most of the time the number of years people expect to be retired will usually fall in the range of 25-33, but your case may be different depending on when it is that you want to retire. In this case, let's say you want to live on $50,000 per year and you expect to be retired for 30 years.

You would then multiply $50,000 by 30 and get a grand total of 1.5 million. This is great because you now have a number that you can aim for.

You'll of course need to think about things such as inflation and healthcare costs when you're determining how much it is that you want to live on per year when you retire. There are of course different ways to go about calculating your retirement, and the best way to go about figuring that out is going to depend on your given situation and goals.

If you're unsure, then it's better to overestimate how much you'll need rather than to underestimate. Yes, I understand that you likely want to retire as soon as you possibly can, however it would be far worse to retire early only to run out of money and possibly have to go back to work.

It'd be far better to maybe take a few extra years to make sure you have plenty of money to be able to live comfortably in retirement without the worry of running out. Of course, at the end of the day, figuring out how much it is that you need to retire is only the start of the journey.

Once you figure out how much it is that you need to retire, the next thing you'll need to do is actually get the money in order to be able to retire. That's the hard part and it's something that most Americans are struggling with today.

Most people don't know exactly where to go when it comes to saving enough for retirement. That's why the rest of this book is going to be dedicated to some of the best methods for helping you retire in a timely manner.

If your goal is to retire early, then you're going to have to be especially diligent with some of the advice found in this book. Yes, you're going to have to be diligent when it comes to how much of your income you're spending. You also might have to consider increasing your income depending on how ambitious your goals are.

That's not something you should be intimidated by though if it'll allow you to retire early. The main point is that once you know when it is that you want to retire and how much it is that you need to retire, then you need to stay focused and pursue the goal with everything you have.

Chapter 2: The Correct Retirement Mindset You Need to Have to See Success

This is one of the most important if not the most important chapter in the book. It's not even talking about specific money tactics, but the way in which you think about money.

This is critically important because I don't want to simply tell you to do this or do that. Retiring early isn't as simple as me telling you what to do and you going out and doing it.

It might seem like it's that simple but it isn't because there's a lot of psychology involved when it comes to money. A simple case in point is that most people know they should take saving for retirement more seriously yet they don't.

To think of it in another way, I could give the same advice to two different people and then end up with two different results. The reason for this would have to do with the mindset of the individuals.

One person might struggle to implement the advice because of his current beliefs or because he's a compulsive spender. On the other hand, the other person might be able to follow through with everything just fine and see success.

The advice was the same, therefore the only difference between these two people was their mindset. In this chapter, we're going to dive deep into the human mind and figure out why it is that some people are able to retire early and why most struggle. Let's dive in...

How Do You View Yourself?

The first thing that I want to talk about here is something known as the self-image. This can make or break your financial success.

The self-image is essentially how you view yourself in regards to different areas of your life. For example, one person might be short and his height affects his confidence in his sales job.

He always feels as if he doesn't get sales because of his height. Then there could be someone else who's also short, but he's glad that he's short because he wants to become a jockey.

These are two different people who are both short, yet one is happy about it and the other one isn't. To use another example, if someone who's broke or is in a bad financial situation woke up tomorrow and found 20 million dollars in his bank account, he'd be pretty happy about it right?

On the other hand, if a multi-billionaire woke up and found that he had *only* 20 million dollars to his name, then he'd be greatly disturbed. You might think that the only reason the multibillionaire would be upset about this is that he lost a lot of his money overnight.

Yes of course that's a valid reason he'd be upset, but it more so has to do with the fact that he views himself as a multibillionaire, not a multimillionaire. The image he has in his mind of who he is isn't consistent with reality any longer.

The multibillionaire who lost a sizable amount of his money would work tirelessly until he got his net worth back into the billions where he believes that his net worth belongs. The other person who was completely broke and discovered 20 million dollars in his bank account would soon enough blow it.

The reason for this is because he views himself as a poor individual. He's always believed that money is hard to come by because of phases he's been told his whole life such as "Money doesn't grow on trees."

He'll subconsciously begin to sabotage the money without even realizing it. If you don't believe someone could blow through millions of dollars in a few years timespan, then look no further than lottery winners.

There's something known as the lottery curse because 70% of lottery winners will go broke within a few years of winning the lottery (3). Often times their lives will become worse after they win the lottery.

One of the main reasons people aren't able to keep the money is because of their self-image. They have a deep subconscious believe about how much money they should have and about how much money they're worthy of having.

Once they get a big influx of money (such as from winning the lottery), their self-image will gradually begin to pull things back and correct the financial situation to where things are in alignment with their current beliefs.

On the other hand, if the multibillionaire won the lottery, then there's a very small chance that he'll lose the money. His financial set point when it comes to money is set well above the millions that he won in the lottery.

The thing is though, we all have a financial set point that we're comfortable with whether we realize it or not. For instance, someone might be comfortable as long as he has $3,000 in his savings account.

If his savings account were to drop significantly below that to let's say $1,500 due to something such as car repairs, then he would start to feel uncomfortable, save more, and spend less so he could get back up to $3,000.

The interesting thing though is what would happen if he got his hands on some extra money. Let's say he gets a nice Christmas bonus of $2,000. Rather than put all of that money in his savings account, he spends most of it on a new T.V. and stereo system.

The logical thing to do would've been to save the money (especially if he's trying to retire early), but remember his financial set point is $3,000 not $5,000. Overall everything averages out to $3,000 in savings.

When he has more money, he'll find a way to spend it. Conversely, when he has less money, he'll find a way to get things back to where they need to be.

Think of it like a thermostat. Imagine this individual's financial thermostat is set to 65 degrees. When things start to dip below that number the heater will come on and start to raise the temperature back up.

However, when the temperature goes above that, the air conditioner will come on and lower the temperature back down to 65 degrees. Right now think about what you have the temperature set to on your financial thermostat.

In the next section, I'll share with you tips you can use to help change the temperature if you're currently not satisfied with it. Now that you're aware of the self-image, I hope you can see how majorly important it is for you to be able to retire early.

If deep down you believe that you can't retire until you're 65, then your subconscious mind will find a way to make that happen. If you start seeing some success that would allow you to retire any sooner than that, you'll start to sabotage yourself without even realizing it. With this being the case, what are some things you can do to change your self-image?

How Can You Change Your Self-Image?

You've already taken the first step to change your self-image and that's to become aware of it. Most people have no clue what the self-image is and it therefore controls their lives without them even realizing what force is at play.

Even with this being the case, having awareness every now and then isn't enough. You need to be aware of your self-image as often as possible. It's when you forget about it, that it'll sneak in and ruin your progress.

Remember these beliefs you have about money, being introverted or extroverted, your level of health, and many other things have been planted in your mind years ago. And these ideas have been reinforced over and over again for years.

Simply knowing what the self-image is and forgetting about it won't do you any good. It's going to take a lot of awareness, practice, and patience to root out these beliefs that we hold deep inside our subconscious mind.

Yes, awareness is the first step, but what can you do to become more aware more often? The first thing you can do is set a reminder on your phone.

Have it go off at a certain time of the day. For instance, the reminder could go off first thing in the morning when you wake up and you could have another reminder go off right before bed.

It would just need to be a simple message saying something like, "Remember Your Financial Set Point." Or you could put your new financial set point in the message.

For example, "Your Financial Set Point is to Have $10,000 in Your Savings Account." Another thing you could do is to write similar messages down on paper and put them in places where you'll regularly see them such as in your bedroom or your desk at work.

This might seem like a silly thing to do, but it'll help keep this on the front of your mind. You're much more likely to remember something if you write it down.

Think of it like shopping at a grocery store without a list. You're much more likely to forget something you needed if you don't write it down and look at it regularly.

Once you do that and become more aware of your self-image, the next thing you must do is question the existing belief. For example, if you want to retire early, but you believe that you won't be able to retire until you're 65, then ask yourself if that's really true.

What you'll see is that you more than likely have some limiting beliefs that are holding you back. If I asked you, is it possible for someone to retire before the age of 65, you would probably answer yes.

However, you might not believe that's it's possible *for you* to retire before you're 65. This could be because of the industry you work in, your background, or something else you believe makes you special and is the reason why you can't retire early.

You need to dig deeper and question those limiting beliefs. For instance, let's say that your parents and grandparents didn't retire until they were all 65 or older. Therefore, you believe that it won't be possible to retire before you're 65 years old.

You'd need to question if that really has to be the case. Ask yourself, was it possible that the 2 generations before me weren't able to retire early because they had the wrong information when it came to finances?

If so, then could you do things differently if you had the right information (which you now will be able to thanks to reading this book)? The answer to that would of course be yes, you could do things differently and get a different result because of it.

All you need to do is dig deep and question every limiting belief that you have about the topic at hand. Don't skip out on this, and casually say "Yeah I can retire before I'm 65."

That's only scratching the surface and it won't change your core beliefs. You must flesh out all of your limiting beliefs when it comes to money and try to think about where these ideas originally came from.

It's not until you're able to do this that anything will be able to change. You have to pinpoint where you got these ideas from in the first place, think about what it was that made you believe it, and then ask yourself if that's still the case today.

More than likely it won't be. You bought into this information because you probably didn't know any better at the time.

You could've been a child and if an authority figure such as your parents or schoolteachers told you something, you probably assumed it was true without questioning it.

Once you've done that, the next thing you need to do in order to help improve your self-image is to face reality. Really take a hard look at your financial situation and face anything you've been hiding from head-on.

For example, most people will look at their bank accounts as little as they possibly can. If they know they have the money for something, they'll spend it, and they'll only check their bank account when they have to.

That's when they'll realize how grim their financial situation is, but they hate being reminded of that so they'll go back to ignoring it again. Basically, people try to sweep their problems under the rug and forget about them rather than face them head-on.

You can't be like that if you want to retire early. You need to take a hard look at where you're currently at. Look and see when it is that you want to retire and look at how much money you currently have to be able to do that.

If it's less than it needs to be, the situation isn't going to get any better by ignoring it. If you do that, then you might not be able to retire when the time comes because you weren't willing to face the music so to speak.

This might seem like an obvious tip, but it's something most people don't do. We'll ignore our problems until they pop up again later only to be worse than ever before.

We ignore our health until we get a serious disease. We ignore our finances for as long as we can.

We put off having hard conversations with friends and family. All of this can be fixed if you simply acknowledge the problem for what it is and then face it straight on rather than running away from it.

What you'll find is that the problem isn't that scary once you face it. The idea of the problem and the agony you create within yourself thinking about the worst possible outcomes is far worse than actually dealing with the issue.

So if right now, you're not in the best situation to retire early, then that's okay. You can at least recognize the problem and use the advice in this book to start turning your situation around.

That's far better than turning 65 for example and realizing that you're nowhere close to being able to retire. The next step you need to take in changing your self-image is to change your standards.

This step is critically important. The reason for this is because we rarely become the people we dream of being one day.

For example, you might have the dream of retiring at a certain age. Or maybe someone else has the dream of becoming a millionaire.

The truth is that these dreams may or may not come true. What will come true is the lowest version of ourselves which we can accept.

For instance, if the lowest version of yourself or your lowest standard is to retire by the time you're 50, then you're going to fight so much harder to make that happen because you don't want to breach your standard.

If you treat things in the opposite manner, where you dream about being able to retire at age 50, then it may or may not happen. It'll happen when you get around to it one day.

And as we all know, that one day probably will never come. To think of it in another way, imagine a bodybuilder who maintains 7% body fat year around.

If something happened and he got up to 12% body fat, then he would immediately start to correct things in order to get back down to 7%. The bodybuilder having 7% body fat is the standard he accepts of himself.

Anything higher than that percentage, and he'll start to workout and diet like crazy so he can get things back to where they belong. Whether you realize it or not, we have standards for everything in our lives—what's acceptable to wear, our level of health, how clean we keep our house, our relationships, and of course of finances.

Therefore, if you're current standards of when it's acceptable to retire are too low, then you need to raise your standards. You need to determine by what age it is that you want to retire at, and then set that as the standard.

If you're off track to achieve that during any point, then you need to start working tirelessly to get things back on track. Start saving more money, get a side hustle, sell things, and do whatever you have to so that you can stay on pace with your new standard.

If your current retirement situation isn't where you'd like it to be, then you must change your norm to where you'd like it to be. Simply setting a new normal though won't be enough.

What you must do is almost become disgusted in a sense with where you're at currently. Loathe at the fact that you're on pace to retire at age 60 when you really want to retire at age 50 for example.

The reality is that if you're completely okay with your financial situation, then there wouldn't be any need to change and you wouldn't even need to be reading this book.

Yet, you're reading this book for a reason, and I suspect that reason is that you want to improve things in regards to your financial situation. That's a good thing!

Don't try to lie to yourself and say everything's okay if it isn't. If you're not happy with where you're at right now, then embrace that so something can be done about it.

Of course, you don't want to take this to the extreme. If you totally hated everything about where you're at right now, then that could lead to you becoming depressed or greatly saddened. Changing your situation overnight isn't going to happen.

Therefore you must strike a balance between accepting where you're currently at and being proud of what you've done to come this far with not being totally satisfied with your current situation. Yes, this is a very delicate balance.

You'll need to take a good look at yourself and see which way you lean towards more. Are you so upset to the point that you're constantly having negative thoughts and you feel like you're never good enough?

If so, then having more self-acceptance and gratitude is the solution for you. On the other hand, do you feel as if you've been too comfortable for too long and as a result of that you haven't made much progress in the past few years?

If that's your situation, then becoming a little bit more dissatisfied at where you're at would probably benefit you. In the end though, you have to realize that your self-image isn't going to change overnight.

However, if you're constantly aware of your self-image and you focus on increasing your standards over time, then you'll start changing things for the better. Simply, be patient and don't get upset if you slip back into old spending habits for example.

Catch yourself and realize you're acting out of old habits that have been ingrained in you for years. All you can do at that point is to try and be better next time.

Setting Goals to Retire Early

Now let's talk about how to properly set goals so that you can retire early. The sad truth is that most people don't set goals.

They have a vague idea in their heads, such as "Yeah I'd like to retire early one day." The thing is though, that's not specific enough.

If that comes true then great, but if it doesn't then whatever. If you want to retire early, then you have to get crystal clear about what it is that you want.

As humans, we're goal seeking whether we realize it or not. Our subconscious minds are constantly looking for the next thing to achieve.

The thing is though that it can be good or bad. If we're constantly filling our minds with negative thoughts, anxiety, and worry then that's what we're going to get more of.

On the other hand, if we're focused on the positive outcomes that we want, then our minds will start to seek out ways to achieve what it is that we desire. Here's the proper way for you to set goals so that you can retire early:

Don't Set Realistic Goals

Many people when they try to set goals fall into the trap of setting "realistic" goals. But what exactly does it mean to be realistic anyway?

Realistic according to who's standards? Many people sadly let the boundaries placed on them by other people influence what they can and can't achieve.

The truth of the matter is that retiring early isn't realistic for most people. Most people will be going down the same path as everyone else, and they don't have much of a chance to retire early.

Conversely, you must be different. You must do different things from the masses in order to achieve the results that they won't be able to.

If you want to achieve realistic goals, then you can do that without even setting a goal in the first place. Therefore, think about what it is that you really want and hold nothing back.

If you're 22 years old right now and you want to retire by the time you're 35, then go out there and do it! Don't let other people's limiting beliefs hold you back on what it is that you truly want and desire for yourself.

A lot of times other people will project their own fears, doubts, and insecurities onto other people. This is because they'd feel uncomfortable if others were able to do something that they couldn't.

Chances are good that your environment and the people you hang out with are determining what you think is possible and isn't possible when it comes to your retirement. I want you to throw all of that out the window.

I want you to think of exactly how you would want things if there were no limits on what you could achieve. That's what you need to do to get down to what it is that you truly want.

Achieving that will give you the most joy and fulfillment. It'll excite you and motivate you to keep on moving forward.

If you set the bar too low, you won't care much about achieving it because you won't even feel like you set the bar to where you wanted it to be at. I mean what else are you supposed to do?

Set goals that are "realistic" for you to achieve, but be saddened by the fact that you want to achieve bigger and better things? There's no such thing as an unrealistic goal, just unrealistic timeframes.

I'm not going to set the bar for you and say that you can't retire before this or that time. You know what financial situation you're in better than I do.

I will tell you though that you're capable of retiring sooner than you might think. It all depends on your starting point of course, but with the proper diligence and game plan, you can pull it off.

You just don't want the negative influence of other people to pull you down and think that you have to wait until you're 65 for you to be able to retire.

Set Multiple Goals in the Future

Once you've gotten the idea of setting realistic goals out of your head, the next thing that you need to do is set multiple goals in the future. Set a goal for when you'd like to retire by and then work backwards from there.

For example, if you're currently 30 years old and you'd like to retire by the time you're 45, then set a goal to retire by the age of 45. That would be a 15-year goal.

You would then work backwards from that point. Set a goal for where you'd like to be 10 years from now so that you'll be on track to retire by age 45.

Then also set a 5-year and 1-year goal as well. After that, set a goal you'd like to achieve a month from now.

Everything should be in proper alignment for you to be able to retire by age 45 if that's your original goal. Once you have all of these goals set, your main focus is going to be on achieving that one-month goal.

The reason for this is because that's close enough in the future where we can see enough of the picture to be able to achieve it. On the other hand, the ultimate 15-year goal of retiring by age 45 is too far off in the future.

There are things you know you need to do to be able to achieve that goal, however because it's so far off into the future it's much easier to put things off and nothing will get done.

This is one of the reasons why most people put off saving for retirement. People know it's important and that they should do it, but because it's so far off into the future they think that they don't have to worry about it right now.

So they keep on delaying and delaying until one day they realize that they don't have enough to retire. That would not be a fun situation to be in.

So what we're going to do instead is focus on hitting short-term goals along the way that'll be in proper alignment with achieving the ultimate long-term goal. And setting a goal one month out is a good short-term goal to shoot for.

It gives you enough time to be able to achieve something meaningful, but it's also not so far off into the future that it's easy to put off doing. Here's a breakdown of what this 30-year old's goals might look like:

Ultimate Goal: Retire by age 45

For the sake of example, let's say this person determines he'll need 3 million dollars saved in order for him to retire by the age of 45. Therefore, the 15-year goal would be to have 3 million dollars saved for retirement by the time he turns 45.

This means that his 10-year goal would be to have 2 million dollars saved by the time he turns 40. And his 5-year goal would be to have 1 million saved by the time he turns 35.

His one-year goal would be to have 200,000 dollars saved for his retirement. Now he could set a one-month goal to store away $16,666 dollars so that he'll stay on track.

Of course this example is a little extreme because we're assuming he hasn't saved anything up to this point and that he's already making quite a bit of money to begin with. You'd of course have to factor in your starting point with anything you have saved up to this point.

For example, if this person already had $500,000 saved for his retirement, then that would completely change things. His 15-year goal of saving 3 million would stay the same, but the numbers would be different.

He'd now only need to save 2.5 million in that same 15-year timespan rather than the full 3 million. In 10 years, he'd need to have roughly 1.6 million saved. In five years, he'd need to have about $833,000 saved.

In one year, he'd need to save approximately $166,666, which would then break down into $13,888 per month. Hopefully, you get the idea of how you're supposed to work backwards from the ultimate goal.

In this example, the person now has clear numbers he knows he needs to go after. Most people don't have this kind of data. That's why they have to take their best guess and then hope for the best, which usually doesn't work out too well.

Make the Goals Clear and With a Deadline

The next thing that you want to do is make your goals clear and be sure to attach a deadline to them. If you don't, then it's easy for your subconscious mind to not take your goals seriously, and you'll keep putting them off until later.

Therefore your goal could be something like this: I save $1,000 for my retirement by March 1st, 2019. This way you've given a clear outcome that you'd like to achieve and you've also attached a deadline for which you'd like to achieve it by.

This is much more powerful than saying something like "save 1,000 dollars." It's also important that you write your goals down by hand.

The reason for this is because that act will make the goal much more real for your subconscious mind. If not, then what you want is just a nice idea in your head.

Writing it down makes the goal a real thing that you actually care about achieving. However, don't write your goal down once and forget about it.

You need to write it down every day so that way it stays fresh on your mind. The best times to usually do this are first thing in the morning and before you go to bed at night.

This way you're goals will be the first thing you think about, and you'll also be thinking about them right before you go to bed allowing your subconscious to think of ways to achieve the goal.

Don't Solely Focus on the Outcome

Yes, the first thing that you need to do is give yourself an outcome that you want to achieve, such as saving $1,000 for your retirement. That's important because that lets you know where it is that you want to go.

However, something that is just as important if not more important is what you're going to do in order to achieve that outcome. Think of the things that you have to do in order to achieve your goal as the road map.

It'll show you what you need to do to reach the final destination, which is the end goal. So in the example of saving $1,000 what is your game plan going to be in order to make that come true?

Maybe your game plan could be to invest more of your paycheck into your retirement account. Or you could cut back on some monthly expenses that you don't use that much and instead put that money towards your retirement.

Finally, you could also do some side hustles and store the extra cash away to help you reach your goal. Essentially you need to come up with a gameplan for what it is that you're going to do in order to achieve the desired outcome.

It's also important to note that once you do have the game plan laid out and ready to go, you want to focus more of your attention on your actions and not the outcome.

The reason for this is that you're not in total control of what outcome will occur. For example, you could have a solid gameplan for how you'll save your next $1,000 for your retirement.

You could then execute on everything perfectly and still fall a little bit short of the goal. That's completely okay if that happens.

If you followed through diligently with your action plan, then you know that you did all that you could. Conversely, if you set the outcome goal, forgot about it, and then didn't come anywhere close to achieving it, then that's not okay.

Having an outcome goal and a gameplan for how you want to achieve it will greatly increase the chances of you achieving that goal. And if you fall short, it won't be that saddening because you'll at least know that you did everything you could in order to achieve the goal.

It's also important to note that you only need to come up with a gameplan for your one-month goal, and maybe your one-year goal if you wanted to do that as well.

The other goals such as the 5 year, 10 year, and ultimate goal are too far into the future for you to be able to accurately assess what it is that you need to do. Not only that, but things will change as time goes on.

So you could set a 5-year gameplan only for it to change completely 2 years into it. It's better to focus more so on what you can do in the present to help change the future.

What's Your Motivation?

The last mindset tip I have for you is to find your motivation. What is it that's motivating you to retire early?

There's some underlying reason whether you see it right now or not. Whenever you have this reason on the front of your mind, you'll have crystal clear focus to be able to keep moving towards your goal.

However, when you forget about why it is that you want to achieve your goal, you might lose motivation and your progress will stagnate. Most people aren't honest with themselves when it comes to their motivation for achieving a certain outcome.

If what you're telling yourself isn't in proper alignment with what's truly motivating you deep down, then you're not going to achieve your goal. For example, when it comes to early retirement, you might tell yourself or other people that the reason why you want to retire early is that you want to travel more.

Let's say though, that deep down the real thing that's motivating you to retire early is so that you can be lazy and watch T.V. all day. If that's your true motivation, then you don't need to run from it.

Embrace it because that's how you'll be able to stay on target with your goals. If not, then you're lying to yourself and you won't care about achieving the goal because the prize at the end isn't going to be that good anyways.

Finding your true motivation is quite simple, all you need to do is ask yourself what's motivating you a couple of times in order to get to the root of what it is that you really want:

What's motivating me to retire early?

I don't want to work anymore.

What's motivating me to not want to work anymore?

I want to live comfortably and do more of the things I like.

What's motivating me to want to live comfortably and do more of the things that I like?

I want to have more freedom to do what I want when I want without my job holding me back.

Now that's so much deeper than the original surface level reason! In this case, the individual wants to retire early so that he can have more freedom.

He desires to be able to do what he wants when he wants to without having to ask his boss first. I'd also be willing to bet that this person doesn't want to wait to be able to have this freedom until he's 65 years old.

That could be too late to be able to truly enjoy his newfound freedom. That's why he wants to get the ball rolling so that he can retire early.

Make sure that you go through this exercise as well in order to discover the deep underlying reason why you want to retire early. Going deep to find your true motivation will make it all the more likely that you'll actually achieve your goals.

Are you enjoying this book so far? If so, please consider leaving a review. Even just a few words would help others decide if the book is right for them!

Chapter 3: Why You Should Increase Your Income to Retire Early

As I said in the very beginning of this book, I'm going to give you advice that's against the norm because retiring early isn't normal. Therefore, you're going to need to be able to do things differently from most people in order to achieve results that they won't be able to get.

The normal advice to go to school, get a job, work hard, and invest in a 401 (k) is great if you want to retire at the standard retirement age of 65. However, since you're reading this book you have different ambitions.

You likely want to retire sooner than that. Of course, how much sooner you want to retire will change how diligent you need to be among other things.

Even with that being the case, there are some core things that you need to start thinking about differently if you plan on retiring early. The first thing you need to think about differently is your income.

Most of us think that our income levels are fixed. For example, an electrician might think that he can only make $50,000 a year because he's an electrician and that's what electricians in his area make.

If he wanted to make more money then he'd have to become a doctor, lawyer, or high-level business executive. That of course isn't true.

There are plenty of ways to make more money regardless of what your current profession is. You might not believe that's true, but it definitely is.

I know this is true because that's how I used to think. I used to think that you had to become a doctor or lawyer if you wanted to make a lot of money and that your job was the only way someone could make money.

When I first heard about the idea of increasing your income I thought that it wasn't possible. Your career path determined how much money you could make and that was that.

Of course, that couldn't be further from the truth. I don't blame you if you think this way because most people do. It's not our fault, this is just how all of us grow up.

We likely grew up with parents and grandparents who thought this was true. And maybe back in their day that was true. However, nowadays with the Internet, things are completely different.

If you want proof of that just look at the book you're currently reading. You ordered the book online and then depending on what format you bought it in, you could start reading it instantly or you had to wait two days to get it shipped to your house.

That's insane and it's something our parents and grandparents likely never would've been able to fathom. However, these beliefs we've been taught don't just come from the people we grew up with.

These ideas are also reinforced when we go to school. In school, we're told time and time again that the key to success is to get good grades.

If you get good grades then you'll get into the best college. And if you get into the best college, then you'll be able to get the best job, which in turn will allow you to make the most money.

If that's the case, then why doesn't school just get straight to the point and teach us about money? Why do we have to jump through all of these hoops in order to start making some money?

The whole point of getting a job in the first place is to make money right? Yet in school we learn nothing about money. Instead, we learn about a bunch of different subjects.

Subjects that do have their own importance no doubt, but the truth is that not everyone will use science in their profession. Not everyone will use geography in their profession.

That's a fact regardless even if your teachers tried to tell you otherwise. On the other hand, everyone will need to use money.

Everyone will need to save for retirement, yet school doesn't help us out in these regards. Well maybe except for in your first-grade class when you learned that a penny is worth a cent, a nickel is 5 cents, etc. but that's about as far as it goes.

That's why it's going to be up to you to learn about money and retirement on your own, which you're certainly doing by reading this book. So it's not your fault if you think a job is the only way you can make money, the educational system beat that idea into your head, and now we have to question if that's really true or not.

Hopefully, by the end of this chapter, you'll have a better understanding of why increasing your income is going to be important if you want to retire early. I'm going to share with you some of the things that helped to change my way of thinking.

You'll learn different things you can do on the side to make more money as well as how to go about making more money at your current job. For now though, I want to tell you why increasing your income is so important if you want to retire early.

Why Increasing Your Income is Critical if You Want to Retire Early

Right now you might be wondering why you should care about increasing your income. Can't you just make the most of what you've got and be good to go?

Well maybe, that all depends on what your goal is for when you'd like to retire and how much it is that you're currently making. Why not do both?

Why not be smart with the money you're currently making and also do your best to increase your income however it is that you can? Most people do neither of these things.

They falsely believe their income level is fixed for reasons we talked about earlier and they're not smart with the money they do have. This obviously creates a disaster down the line when they want to retire, but they can't.

Instead by focusing on increasing your income, you'll be able to give yourself more options. You'll have more flexibility to be able to retire earlier, and you'll also have more money in case of emergencies.

If you don't focus on increasing your income, then you're going to be completely reliant on the amount of money that you're currently making. That of course could be a good thing or bad depending on what your income is at.

Let's say for example, someone makes $30,000 a year. If this person does nothing to increase his income, then when he can retire and what he'll be able to do when he is retired will be limited.

He might not be able to travel as much as he'd like to because he wasn't able to save enough for his retirement. Or worse he might have to retire later than expected because he wasn't able to save enough money per month.

Remember we're going to be doing things differently from most people. In this example, the person who makes $30,000 a year likely thinks he's stuck with making that much.

Therefore he can only save so much per month for his retirement and he has to wait many years until he has enough saved up to finally be able to retire. Conversely, if he would focus on increasing his income, then he would suddenly have more options.

He'd have much more control over when he could retire, and when he does retire then he'll have more freedom as to what he can do. Sounds like a win-win doesn't it?

You no longer have to solely rely on retiring early by squeezing everything you can out of pennies. Sure there's nothing wrong with doing that, but you might as well combine your money saving efforts with increasing your income for the most potent effect.

Let's go ahead and get into some ways to increase your current income.

How to Make More Money at Your Current Job

The first way to go about increasing your income is to increase your salary at your current job. Depending on what industry you're in, you might not think this is possible.

However, what I want you to do is suspend your current beliefs for a moment. I want you to go ahead and act as if you're about to get a raise.

How much harder would you work if you knew you were about to get a raise? Imagine if you were the very best at what it is that you do.

Don't you think you'd get paid more if that's the case? However, if right now you don't believe that working harder or increasing your skill set will have any payoff, then you won't do it.

That's why I want you to go ahead and have a good attitude and act as if you're already going to get a raise. What's the worst that can happen?

You already have to show up to work anyways so you might as well give your best effort. If you don't think it's worth it, trust me I can totally relate.

I used to work a retail job where I got paid $8.60 an hour. I got my first 50 cent raise for signing up the most people to the rewards program.

I was relentless about signing people up. I just did it without even thinking about getting a raise because that was the standard that I held myself to.

Then one day I got called into the office and was told I was getting a raise for the good work that I had done. I was surprised and happy of course.

Afterwards though, I started to develop a negative attitude. I complained about having to sign up people for the rewards program. I complained to my friends about how I was at a dead-end job.

My numbers on the sign-ups for the rewards program went down. Needless to say, I didn't end up getting another raise before I ended up quitting that job.

Looking back on it, having a better attitude definitely would've changed things. I could have stayed diligent with the rewards program, and looked to move into a management position.

From there I could've become a general manager and possibly even moved to a corporate position had I been focused on improving the quality of my work. Saying that I was at a dead-end job was a lie I was telling myself so that I wouldn't have to improve.

Even if the job I had ultimately wasn't the right fit for me, I still could've done my best work and taken promotions wherever possible. It would've been easier for me to transition to a job that better suited me had I performed my best work.

Therefore step number one when it comes to making more money at your current job is to always have a good attitude and perform your best work. You never know who's watching you.

The next thing you want to do to get a promotion at work is to be prepared. You don't want to walk into your boss's office and straight up ask for a raise if there's no good reason for you to get one.

Many people believe they deserve a raise simply because they've been working at a company for a certain number of years. Yes, loyalty is important, but it's not the most important thing.

The most important thing is value. What kind of value do you bring to the company?

If you've been working for the same company for the past 15 years, yet you still have the same skill set as when you started, then why is it that you deserve a raise?

I'm not trying to be harsh, I'm just trying to prepare you for an objection your boss might have. That's why it's critical you come in prepared.

Show your boss the data and numbers behind how it is that you've been able to help the company. Maybe the company has been able to increase sales by a certain percentage thanks to the work you've done.

Have all of the numbers and proof ready to go when you ask for a raise. In my case, I would've shown how consistent my rewards program sign-ups were and brought statistics about how rewards members buy more than non-rewards members.

Make your case as compelling as you possibly can. Many times this means you're going to have to delay gratification by doing stellar work for months on end in order to make it a no-brainer for why you deserve a raise.

The final tip I have for you in regards to getting a raise is to ask for it at the right time. You want to ask your boss for a raise when he's fresh.

This means either in the morning soon after the work day has started or soon after lunch. You don't want to ask your boss for a raise towards the end of the workday.

At this point, your boss is fatigued from a long day at work and you're less likely to get a raise. Believe it or not, this is a real thing that was shown in cases of parole hearings.

A study showed that people who had their parole hearings in the early morning or right after lunch were much more likely to get out on parole compared to people who had their hearings at the end of the day or right before lunch (4).

That's crazy to think about, and fortunately you can use this information to help you get a raise at your current job.

How to Increase Your Income with Side Hustles

You're not only limited to making money from your current job. There are also plenty of different ways you can make money on the side from your main job.

The first way you can go about increasing your income is to sell off stuff you don't need anymore. You can have a garage sale or sell your items online, which is what I prefer because it's a lot easier to do.

If you're experiencing some resistance to this, that's okay and it's actually to be expected. The reason for this is because of something known as the endowment effect.

It basically states that we value things more once we own them. For example, let's say you're cleaning your house one day and you stumble across a rare baseball card that's worth $1,000.

You decide to frame it and keep it in your house. Then let's imagine a different scenario where you don't own the card, but you see it in a card shop one day selling for $1,000.

You think that price is ridiculous and you'd never pay that kind of money for a baseball card. The thing is though that you're essentially paying that price by keeping the card in the other scenario.

So what can you do in order to overcome the endowment effect? The first thing that helps is to simply be aware of it.

Most people have no clue why they value certain things they own so much, and having that awareness is the first step to overcoming it. Secondly, ask yourself when the last time it was that you used the item.

For example, in the case of the baseball card, you could ask yourself how much do you really care about it? How long has it been sitting in a shoebox under your bed for?

We don't use most of our possessions on a day-to-day basis. A lot of the things we own will go months or years before we feel the need to use them.

By being honest with yourself about how much you really use/need the item will help make things easier to sell it. Finally, you can start off by selling something small.

Once you sell that item, you'll realize that it wasn't so bad and you didn't really need it that much to begin with. Then you can work your way up to selling things that might be harder to let go of.

Don't feel as if you have to get rid of everything at once. Just make sure you actually think about selling some of your possessions off.

It's an easy way to get some extra money, and it would be a total bummer if not selling these items was the difference between you retiring early or retiring later than you want to.

Now let's talk about other things you can do to increase your income. The first would be to either get a part-time job on the side or you could do something that allows you to be more flexible with your hours such as participating in a ridesharing company or food delivery service.

Either way both of these options are a great way to be able to increase your income. Yes, you'll be working very hard, but it'll all be worth it when you can retire early.

You're essentially putting in the work up front so that you won't have to do it later. If you decide to increase your income by driving for a ridesharing company, then you'll get to be flexible and choose when and how much you want to work.

However, the downside to that is that you won't be held accountable. You can easily not drive on the side if you're feeling tired and you won't have to deal with any consequences.

On the other hand, if you get a part-time job on the side, then you'll be held accountable to show up by your boss. Be honest with yourself about whether or not you need accountability in order to get the job done.

Of course, you don't have to get another part-time job if you don't want to. There are plenty of other ways to make money.

Remember what I said earlier, the Internet has completely changed the game. Thanks to the Internet you now have plenty of options available to you as to how you can go about making some extra money on the side.

Not only that, but a lot of these things can be automated to where you're making money when you're not even technically working. You'd create a product for example, and then it can sell online 24/7 without you having to do anything.

You put in the hard work up front and then your product will start working hard for you. So how can you go about doing this?

Well like I said, there are plenty of different ways to make money online. I won't be able to cover every way that you can make money online, but hopefully I've piqued your curiosity enough to look into it more if this sounds like a good option for you.

One of the most popular ways to make money online is to sell a digital product such as an ebook or video course. Essentially you'll make a course about a topic you know a lot about and then sell it to other people.

Since the product is completely digital, you don't have to worry about any inventory, logistics with shipping, or anything like that. Digital products are usually pretty cheap and easy to make, and best of all you won't have to worry about any extra costs like you would with physical products.

The thing is that you can make a digital product around just about anything. Let's say you're really passionate about riding horses.

You could make a digital product about riding horses and then sell it to people online. You could make a video course and in the course, you could show people how to properly mount and dismount from the horse.

How to saddle a horse. Safety tips. How to work up to riding at faster paces on the horse. How to halt and turn etc.

And you don't have to be the world's greatest expert to teach online either. As long as you know valuable information that your target audience wants, then you'll be good to go because that's all that people care about!

In fact, if you were the world's best horse rider for example, then beginners might not be able to relate to you as well. Just ask yourself, "What's a topic that I could talk about for hours on end without even noticing the time going by? What's something my friends and family come to me and ask advice for?"

These are good places to start! Once you've made your product, the next thing you need to be able to do is market it.

There are plenty of different ways you can go about doing this. For example, you could start a blog where you share with people various tips on the subject you're talking about.

Then on the blog, you can ask people to sign up for your email list, which is where you can promote your product. You can also start a video channel as well if you prefer making videos over writing.

You can promote your product via social media as well. The point is that there are a lot of possibilities out there for you to be able to make money.

You just have to be open to the idea of it because nobody tells us about making money online in school. Regardless of what it is that you want to do, definitely look into ways to increase your income because you'll have more options when it comes to your retirement gameplan and who doesn't want that?

Chapter 4: What You Need to Know About 401(k)'s and IRA Accounts

Now let's go ahead and talk about your actual retirement accounts. These are what most people are going to be relying on when it comes to retirement so it's important that you know a thing or two about them.

The sad thing is that most people have no clue about how a 401(k) works for example. They just know that a percentage of their check goes into their retirement fund and they leave it at that. You must be better than that because you want to retire early. Here's a breakdown of what 401(k)s and IRAs are:

What is a 401(k) and IRA?

A 401(k) is a retirement investment account offered to you by your for-profit employer. Government jobs or non-profits offer something known as a 403(b).

For the most part, these retirement plans are the same except for the fact that in the case of the 403(b) the employer can save on some administrative costs. I'll be focusing most of the attention on the 401(k) as that's what most people will be dealing with.

Just know that if you're dealing with a 403(b), the same basic advice for a 401(k) will likely still apply to you in the majority of cases. With that being said, when you get a new job, the company will offer you the option to enroll in their 401(k).

Once you enroll, you'll select a certain percentage of your income that you'll contribute to the fund each month. So for example, if your salary is $75,000 you might choose to contribute 6% of your monthly income to your 401(k).

You'd be making around $6,250 per month of which you'd then contribute $375 to your 401(k). The cool thing is that most employers will offer you a match up to a certain point.

For example, an employer might match you dollar per dollar up to the first 6% that you contribute. Continuing on with our example, this means that your employer would contribute $375 per month on top of what you're already contributing.

This of course isn't to say that you can't contribute more to your 401(k) then 6%, but most companies will only match up to the first 6%. And of course, companies will vary on their contribution.

Some might only offer to match 50 cents on the dollar for the first 6%. In this example, that would mean the employer would offer $187.50 per month on top of your contribution.

You'll need to look and see what kind of employer match your company offers or if they even offer one to begin with. From there, you'll know what you need to do in order to maximize it.

For example, if your company does match up to the first 6%, then it wouldn't be wise to contribute less than 6% if you could at all help it. Using the example of making $75,000 per year, let's say you only want to invest 5% of your income into the 401(k) plan.

That's $312.50 per month of which your company would match. If it's a dollar per dollar match, then that means you're missing out on an extra $62.5 per month from your employer.

That might not seem like a lot, but keep in mind that this is essentially free money that will be invested and compounding over time. Over the years of your career that could add up to make a huge difference.

That's definitely something you don't want to be missing out on especially if you're trying to retire early. On top of this, you also have traditional 401(k)'s and ROTH 401(k)'s.

The main difference between them has to do with taxes. In a traditional 401(k) you're essentially making your contribution with a tax deferment. In a traditional 401(k), let's say you made $75,000 and you contributed $4,500 to your 401(k) plan for the year. That money will be used as a deduction and you'll only pay taxes on an income of $70,500 rather than 75,000.

In a traditional 401(k) you won't pay any taxes on the money in the account until you withdraw it once you're retired. The amount you pay in taxes will be determined by your current income bracket when you retire.

It doesn't matter if you started in a low tax bracket when you first started contributing to your 401(k). All that matters is where you end up when you retire, and all of your retirement money will be taxed at the same rate.

With a ROTH 401(k) account you're paying the tax upfront on any money that you invest. You of course won't be able to deduct your 401(k) contribution off of your taxable income, but the ROTH does have its advantages.

For example, most people will earn more money as they get older. This makes sense because as time goes on, you should be increasing your skills and getting promotions.

With that being the case, by using a ROTH 401(k), you'll be able to pay those taxes upfront while you're still in a lower tax bracket. This could result in some huge tax savings over the years depending on the situation you're in.

For most people, this is the better way to go as their income will increase over the years. The ROTH 401(k) will allow people to pay taxes along the way while their income isn't as high as it'll hopefully be one day in the future.

For some people though, the traditional 401(k) will make more sense if you're already a high-income earner and you think you might end up in a lower tax bracket when you retire.

Finally, the last couple of basic things you need to know about 401(k)'s are the yearly amount you can contribute and when you can withdrawal your money. As of the writing of this book, you can contribute up to $18,500 per year into your 401(k).

That should be plenty for most people, but that of course all depends on how ambitious your retirement goals are. And you can't withdraw your money until your 59.5 years old.

Well, you can withdraw the money, but you're going to get slapped with a 10% early withdrawal penalty. That's certainly a lot of money especially if you've diligently been investing in this account to retire early.

Imagine if you had 2 million saved for your retirement and then you had to pay a $200,000 penalty just to get access to your own money. That's definitely a big bummer especially if your idea of early retirement starts before the age of 59.5.

Now that we've covered the 401(k) in depth, let's talk about the IRA. IRA stands for individual retirement account.

As of the writing of this book in 2018, you're allowed to contribute $5,500 per year to your IRA account if you're under the age of 50. If you're 50 or older you're allowed to contribute up to $6,500 per year to your IRA account.

In 2019, these numbers are expected to increase to $6,000 and $7,000 per year respectively. And just like with the 401(k), there are two different kinds of IRAs—traditional and ROTH.

In a traditional IRA, you're going to defer paying taxes on the money that you contribute to the retirement account until you're ready to start withdrawing it. With a ROTH IRA, you're going to pay taxes upfront before the money is placed into the retirement account.

Just like traditional and ROTH 401(k), the traditional and ROTH IRA both have their pros and cons. The one that's better for you will of course depend on your situation.

As with the 401(k), the ROTH option is going to be better for you if you plan on retiring in a higher tax bracket than you're currently in. The traditional IRA is going to be better if you're already making a good amount of money or if you plan on retiring in a lower tax bracket.

When it comes to IRA's though, there is one cool thing about using a ROTH IRA as opposed to a traditional IRA. With the ROTH IRA, you're actually allowed to withdraw any money you've contributed without penalty before the age of 59.5 as long as the ROTH IRA account is at least 5 years old.

However, you still won't be able to withdraw the earnings from what you've contributed before the age of 59.5 unless you want to pay the 10% penalty. There are some exceptions to this however, such as if you're buying your first house, paying for college either for yourself or your children, or certain medical expenses.

For the most part though, if you want the earnings you've made from your ROTH IRA before you're 59.5, then you're going to have to pay a penalty. So what do I mean when I say that you can withdrawal contributions you've made but not earnings?

Well, let's say that over a 10 year period you put $30,000 into your ROTH IRA account from the money you made from your job. And let's say you invested that $30,000 into stocks.

The stocks allowed you to make an additional $20,000 for a grand total of $50,000 in the account. You'd be allowed to withdraw the $30,000 because that's what you originally contributed to the account.

You wouldn't be able to take out the earnings from your investments, which in this case would be $20,000 unless you want to pay the penalty. This is different from a ROTH 401(k) because in a ROTH 401(k), you're not allowed to make withdrawals even from your contributions without paying the penalty. As long as you're still working for the company providing the 401(k) or if you're under the age of 59.5, then you're options are limited with the ROTH 401(k).

There are a few rare exceptions to this such as going on disability, but by and large, there aren't many ways to get around the penalty if you want to withdraw early from a ROTH 401(k). Of course though, there are some benefits to the 401(k) that the IRA won't be able to offer you.

For instance, the yearly contribution limit to the 401(k) is roughly 3 times as high as the IRA. Not only that but with the 401(k), you'll potentially be able to take advantage of an employer match depending on what your company offers.

In regards to the IRA since it's an individual account, it's all on you to make contributions. In an IRA, it's also up to you to decide how you want to invest your money.

With a 401(k), your money is usually going to be invested into mutual funds that will consist of different stocks and bonds. With an IRA, you can choose whatever it is that you want to invest your money in.

This could be anything from exchange-traded funds, stocks, bonds, unit investment trusts, gold, silver, oil, real estate, and mutual funds among other things.

There are a few exceptions to this as far as what you're not allowed to invest in such as life insurance and collectibles. Collectables would include things such as stamps, baseball cards, or coins for example.

So What's Better the 401(k) or IRA?

Now you're probably wondering what the better route is— 401(K) or IRA? Well, this is all of course going to depend on your current situation and your retirement goals.

For example, if you're starting a new job and that company offers an amazing 401(k), then you might not want to pass up on that. This would be especially true if you plan on contributing more than $5,500 per year to your retirement account which is the current limit for the IRA.

However, you also have to consider when it is that you want to retire. If you want to retire before the age of 59.5 and start withdrawing your money early, then you're more than likely going to have to take the 10% penalty hit with the 401(k).

A 401(k) could also be a better option for you if you're not sure of what you should invest in. In a managed 401(k) account the investments will be taken care of for you usually by the investment manager for the company you work for.

This is great if you don't want to worry about what to invest in or deal with managing your portfolio. However, this of course won't come without a price.

There will be fees involved such as investment advisory fees and shareholder transaction costs. These are all things you'll need to take into consideration when you decide which retirement path is best for you.

The IRA is great if you know what you want to invest in and if you don't mind managing it along the way. It'll help save you on fees, which can add up over time.

Of course though, you still have the option of hiring someone to manage your IRA account if you want to so it's flexible. More than likely though, you might already be investing into a 401(k) or IRA.

If that's the case, then you'll need to take everything into consideration to see what your next move should be. For example, you could currently be investing your money into your company's 401(k) plan.

However at the end of the year, you may be leaving for a new job in which case you may decide it's best to roll over that money into an IRA account. The point is to be diligent and really take a hard look at your current situation.

See if you're on track to hit your retirement goal and see if any changes need to be made. For example, maybe you're currently contributing $3,000 a year to a ROTH IRA account.

After taking a hard look at your financial goals, you decide it's best to cut back on some other expenses so that you can now contribute $4,000 per year to your IRA account.

Most people aren't willing to do this and that's why their retirement situation is a complete mess. They aren't willing to face the music and realize that something needs to change if they're going to be able to retire when they want to.

As I've said throughout this book, if you want to retire early then you must be different from the masses. Most people have no clue about what's going on in their retirement account.

They might've set up a 401(k) years ago and then completely forgotten about it. They'll just hope that enough money is in there when they want to retire.

That's not a good idea if you want to have a comfortable retirement. So make sure you take some time to really think about and decide what the best option is for your situation.

Different 401(k) Rollover Options

A common situation that people find themselves in is when they leave their current employer for a new job. You might have a 401(k) plan with your current employer and decide to leave for a new job.

In these circumstances, you'll need to decide what it is that you want to do with your 401(k). Thankfully you do have some options, and the best one will likely depend on your given situation.

The first thing you can do when you leave your current employer is to cash out your 401(k). This is rarely a good idea.

If you're under the age of 59.5, then this means that you likely won't be able to get around that 10% penalty. And if you were using a traditional 401(k) then you're no longer going to be able to defer the taxes owed on the money.

You're going to have the pay the taxes on the money before you get access to it. Like I said, in the majority of cases, this probably isn't going to be a good idea.

However, if you find yourself in a pinch financially you do have this option available if you need it. The next option you have is to leave your 401(k) with your old employer.

The benefit of doing this has to do with something known as the rule of 55. This rule basically states that if you leave your job, are fired, or are laid off and you're between the ages of 55 and 59.5, then you can withdrawal from your 401(k) without penalty.

This is a pretty good deal if you ever find yourself in this situation. However, most of the time people will not be in this situation so it won't make sense for a lot of people.

It's also important to note that this only applies to the money from the 401(k) with the employer you're leaving once you're between the ages of 55 and 59.5. If you have money that's in a different 401(k) or 403(b) from a former employer that you left before the age of 55, then that money will still be subjected to the 10% penalty.

Also if you rolled over any money from a former 401(k) into an IRA, then the rule of 55 doesn't apply. The rule of 55 only applies to 401(k) plans and not IRAs.

Again like I said, this option won't apply to most people in the majority of cases, but it's still nice to be aware of all of your options. Thirdly you can rollover your old 401(k) plan into a new 401(k) if your new employer allows it.

If you're in a traditional 401(k), then this will allow you to still be able to defer taxes. And you'll still only have to manage one retirement account instead of two.

This option could potentially have you delay required minimum distributions (RMD) as well. An RMD is essentially the minimum amount of money that you must start withdrawing from your account once you reach the age of 70.5.

However, if you're still working when you reach this age, then you can delay taking the required minimum distribution with the money in your 401(k) from your current employer. Essentially, if you were to rollover your old plan into your new employer's plan, then you could delay RMDs for a larger portion of your money if you plan on working past the age of 70.5.

If you left your old 401(k) at your former employer and didn't roll it over, then you would have to start withdrawing the money from that account once you reach the age of 70.5. Of course, this is a book about retiring early so you likely aren't interested in working past the age of 70.5, but it's still nice to know all of your options.

Finally, you can rollover your 401(k) with your former employer to an IRA. This is what most people will typically do when they leave a company.

The main reason for this is because rolling over into an IRA will give you more options for what it is that you can invest in. Of course, you'll have to decide if you want to roll over into a traditional or ROTH IRA.

If you're going from a traditional 401(k) to a ROTH IRA, then you'll have to pay taxes before the money can be placed in the IRA. If you want to keep deferring the tax payment, then you can roll over from a traditional 401(k) to a traditional IRA. The best option will, of course, depend on your current situation and retirement goals.

Chapter 5: How to Save More Money to Make Early Retirement a Reality

When it comes to retiring early, there are two different ways you can go about it—saving more and/or making more. In this book, I'm going to talk about ways that you can do both, but typically the easier thing to do in most cases is to work on spending less and saving more.

Think about it like a ship. Making more money is like you adding more size to the ship, you make it more robust.

It can carry more things and it's harder to take down. However, how much you spend/save is like having a hole in your ship.

It doesn't matter how much you make if all you do is spend it all each month. That hole will continue leaking water into the ship and you'll have to plug it up in order to stop it.

Using a bucket to keep pouring the water overboard won't do you any good. The core problem is still there. That's why the phrase, "it's not what you make, it's what you manage" matters so much.

You could be making a sizable income each and every month, but none of that matters if you spend it all. That hole in your ship is still there trying to sink you and you're struggling to stay afloat.

And often times it can be little holes in the ship that we don't even notice. I'm talking about small things here and there that add up over time to make the difference between being able to retire early and not.

For example, the dinners out, $5 lattes every morning, and just other little expenses that we don't seem to notice at first are what hurt us the most in the long run.

It's not until we really take a hard look at things sometimes that we notice a hole in our financial ship that needs to be fixed. Don't get me wrong here, I'm not saying that if you want to retire early you can never enjoy your life and must be a total miser.

However, you do have to realize that in order for you to achieve your goal, then certain sacrifices must be made. Different sacrifices will have to be made for different people in different situations.

Maybe you can get away with a $5 latte every morning, but your friend who's also trying to retire early won't be able to. It really comes down to your specific financial situation and what your retirement goals are.

In this chapter, I'm going to share with you common things that eat up more of people's money than they expect. And I'm also going to show you how these expenses cost you more than what's shown on the receipt.

This is the First Thing You Must Do to Start Saving Money

The first thing you must do in order to save more money is to become aware. You need to look at your bank statements and see exactly where your money is going.

Doing this can be very alarming, and that's why most people don't do it. They're afraid of what they might find and they don't want to face reality.

Take a look at the statements for the past few months and see if you notice any patterns. Are you going out to the bars a lot? Did you go on a shopping spree?

What kind of monthly subscriptions do you have? These are all things you need to take notice of so that you can fix them.

And the best way to be able to be better about not making unnecessary purchases in the future is to set up a budget. A budget will essentially set the boundaries for what you can and can't spend money on, and how much money you can spend on certain things.

It's essentially as if you're setting up bumpers when you're going bowling. These bumpers won't allow you're spending to go past a certain point assuming that you actually stick to your budget.

If you don't have a budget, then it's as if you're bowling without the bumpers. You're spending can get completely out of control and your bowling ball can go in the gutters so to speak.

Setting up and sticking to a budget doesn't have to be that hard either. The first thing you need to do to set up a budget is to figure out what your monthly income is.

That will set the parameters for everything else it is that you're going to do. After you determine that, the next step is to figure out your fixed costs.

This would include things such as your electric and water bill, mortgage, car payment, credit card payments, etc. Yes, there are going to be other costs you have every month, but for now, we just want to deal with the fixed costs that you're going to be paying every month.

Once you figure out your fixed monthly bills, then subtract those expenses from your monthly income. After you've taken care of your fixed expenses, you now want to think about your variable expenses.

This would be things such as entertainment, food, and gas for your car among other things. When you're first starting up a budget, it can be hard to determine exactly how much you need to budget for various expenses.

That's why it's a good idea to take your best guess and then adjust as needed. You can get a good idea of how much it is that you might need for food each month by looking at your previous bank statements.

Keep in mind though, that you might've spent more on food than you wanted to before you put a budget into place. Just because you spent $300 a month on food before you put a budget into place doesn't mean that you have to keep spending that amount once the budget is in place.

Instead, start with the ideal and realistic amount that you think you can spend on food each month. Maybe $300 a month was too high and you think you can pull that back to $200 per month. On the other hand, setting a food budget of $0 is unrealistic because you have to eat in order to survive.

After you account for all of this, you should (hopefully) have some money leftover. If you don't have any money left over after accounting for all of your expenses, then you need to take another look at where all of your money is going and see how you can make some adjustments.

The thing is that you want to account for every dollar that you're making. If you don't, then you'll find a way to spend that extra money if it isn't accounted for.

For example, if you have $200 leftover that isn't accounted for in your budget, then it's easier to slip and spend it on a shopping spree. Instead, if you have a plan in place to put that same $200 in savings, then you know you won't be able to go on that extra shopping spree because it's not a part of the budget.

You want to take any leftover money you have after accounting for your expenses and decide what the best plan of action is. The first thing I would recommend doing is putting some money aside each month to put into savings.

If you don't have any money saved, then now would be the best time to start. And I'm talking about a personal savings account here, not any money you would have saved in a 401(k) or IRA.

Yes, the interest you'll earn from the bank from a savings account is negligible, typically less than half a percent per year. However, it's nice to have some money saved up in case of an emergency.

If your car breaks down and it's going to cost a decent chunk of change to fix, then it's nice to have the money ready to go to not have to worry about it. This is far better than what most people do who live paycheck to paycheck.

If their car broke down, they'd likely have to use a credit card to get it fixed. Then they might fall behind on the payments, which will allow interest to start occurring and then a vicious cycle will start.

Therefore, it's wise to put some money aside for emergencies that you can't foresee happening. And it doesn't have to be a lot either.

Just start with what you can even it's just 5%-10%. That's way more than most Americans are saving and it'll add up over time better than you might think.

After you've determined a monthly amount that you want to set aside for savings, you now need to consider what you want to do with the rest of your leftover money. This is where things can get a bit interesting.

The goal is to retire early, therefore you need to look and see if it's possible for you to contribute more of your monthly income towards your retirement plans such as your 401(k) or IRA.

This is a great thing to consider because the money will come out before you even see it, which won't allow you to spend it on frivolous items. And most importantly doing this will allow for more compound interest and allow you to retire early, which is the name of the game here.

However, the other thing you need to consider are any debts that you have. What kind of credit card debt do you have? How much more do you owe on your house and/or car?

The last thing you want to happen is to have excessive interest occur from credit cards for example because you're not able to pay them off in a timely manner. The interest on credit cards is typically going to be far more than any money you're making from your retirement account.

Therefore it makes sense to focus on trying to pay off your high-interest credit cards first before you consider investing more into your retirement account. Don't worry, I'm going to talk more in-depth about paying off big expenses such as a house, car, and credit cards in another chapter.

For now though, you need to carefully look at the interest rates on your credit cards and see what kind of situation you're in. If you're about to start accruing interest on a particular card, then it would be wise to pay it off as soon as possible to avoid interest.

Even changing up your budget to where you could be saving less per month so you can focus on getting that card paid off would be wise. Credit card debt is something that stifles the dreams of people who want to retire, and we have to stay focused on the goal.

Once you get the high-interest cards paid off, you can then go back to saving the regular amount you allocated for. The best thing you can do with your leftover discretionary income is to put the money where it needs to be right when you get it.

For example, if you get paid once a month and you're starting out by saving 10% of your monthly income, then put that money in savings as soon as you get it. That way you won't be tempted to spend it on something else.

Then if you're using some of your leftover money to pay off a credit card, do it as soon as you get paid. Make saving money or paying certain bills the priority.

If the money is already gone or saved in a separate place, then you can't spend it on something that isn't necessary. The last thing that you'll want to do is make sure that you check your budget regularly.

For example, if you created your budget in a spreadsheet, then make sure you check it daily. Yes, that's right daily!

It does you no good to set a budget and then never look at it again, which is what quite a few people do. However, if you're looking at this every day, then you'll always be aware of the financial situation that you're in.

You'll constantly see how much credit card debt you have for example, and you'll be way more likely to address it rather than to try and forget about it. Most people are in terrible financial situations and they try to ignore their finances as much as possible.

By facing reality and looking at your budget on a daily basis, you'll stay focused on the goal, which is to get your money in check so that you can retire early. All in all though, the best way to get better at budgeting is to practice it.

At first, it might not be that smooth. However, as time goes on, things will get easier and easier. So be patient in the beginning if you're new to this because things will get easier and easier as time goes on.

How to Save Money on Common Expenses

Now that we've talked about setting a budget, the next thing you need to focus on is how you want to go about saving more money. For example, if there are some monthly expenses you could get rid of that would be huge.

You could then start putting that money to better use such as getting out of debt or have more money each month to start saving. Make every dollar count.

Here are some things you should consider to help you save more money:

Tip #1: Keep a Record of Everything You Buy

If you set up a budget, then you're already well on your way to implementing this first tip. By tracking and recording every dollar that you spend, you'll be less likely to spend your money on little purchases here and there.

For example, maybe you're at a gas station and you usually get a soda and some candy before you leave. Normally you'd just swipe your debit card and not think about it.

However, now that you're actually going to have to record that $3 expense in your budget, the effort of going through that may not be worth it. If you take a look at your bank statement, then you might be surprised at how quickly these little purchases can add up.

Getting a few drinks at the bar, eating out a couple of times, and other small monthly expenses can really add up to make the difference between you reaching your goal of early retirement and completely missing it.

Not only will tracking everything you spend make you less likely to spend money on unnecessary things, but it'll also help you become more aware of what you typically want to spend your money on.

This will help you get better and better at knowing where you can improve on things as time goes on. Awareness really is the key to saving more money.

You have to first know exactly where your money is going if you want to fix it. Most people aren't really that aware of their financial situation and that's why it's usually a mess.

They don't see how these little purchases of $9 here or $3 there can really add up to hurt them. And ultimately it can hurt people in multiple ways as you're about to find out.

Tip #2: This is How Much Items Really Cost

From now on, I don't want you to look at the price of how much something costs and think that's all there is to it. For instance, if you're going shoe shopping and you see a pair of shoes priced at $80, I don't want you to think that the shoes cost $80.

In reality, those shoes cost so much more than $80. The reason for this is because of something that is known as opportunity cost.

Opportunity cost is the loss of a potential gain because of a decision that you made. So for example, if you decide to buy that $80 pair of shoes, then that means you're not putting that $80 towards paying off a credit card or in your retirement account.

On the surface, it only seems like $80 so it's not that big of a deal in the grand scheme of things. However, imagine what would happen if instead you invested that same money into something else that could bring about compound interest.

Now instead of spending that $80 on a pair of shoes and never seeing the money again, you're now putting that $80 to work for you. And this is the case with every unnecessary purchase that you make.

It all adds up to cost you more than what the price tag says because you're essentially missing out on the opportunity to invest the money and have it grow. Depending on how young you are, that $80 pair of shoes could really be costing your hundreds when you think of things in terms of opportunity cost.

The sooner you can invest any extra money that you have, the better off you'll be. Thinking of things in this manner might be hard at first or it might even seem unnecessary.

However, I would strongly recommend that you try it out because it'll help give you a better defense against making frivolous purchases. And I'm sure you noticed that these first two tips (and even the next one) are psychological more so than saying to get rid of this or that.

The reason for it is because as humans we tend to buy on emotion more than we should at times. By implementing these first few tips you'll be able to be more conscious of what it is that you're spending your money on, which is the foundation of saving more money.

Tip #3: Limit Impulse Buys

The next tip I have for you is to limit impulse buys. If you've ever bought on impulse before, then I can totally relate to you.

I've bought $60 video games before on a whim only to play them a couple of times. I now regret those purchases and wish that I had that money back.

It can be easy to fall for the hype of something if all of your friends are getting something new. You need to remember to keep the main thing the main thing and that's going to be early retirement.

The first thing you can do to limit impulse buys is to ask yourself why you want this particular item. Do you only want it because all of your friends are getting it?

Would this be something you'd normally want if it wasn't trending right now? Or is the packaging on an item really cool and that could be what's steering you in the direction of buying it?

When that's the case, just imagine the item in a plain and boring package and see if you still like it as much. Asking yourself these types of questions is very powerful because it can help make you think logically.

Most of the time when we buy on impulse we're buying on emotion not off of sound logic. The other thing you can do to limit your impulsive spending is to wait a week and see if you still want that item.

For example, if you want a new accessory for your smartphone, then wait a week and see if you still want it. Having a cool off period is a good way to be able to judge if you actually want something.

Of course, it's important to note that you need to limit exposure to this item you want during this weeklong period in any way that you can. If you're still seeing commercials for the item or listening to your friends brag about how cool this particular thing is, then you're not really cooling off and you're more likely to buy it.

Tip #4: Cut Monthly Expenses Where Possible

Once you've taken care of the first three tips, you've now laid a foundation from which you can build upon. It's now time to focus on some ways that you can cut back on your expenses.

The first thing you need to take a look at is your monthly expenses that aren't necessities. This can really add up quickly.

Let's say for example you're spending $10 per month on a music subscription service and another $10 per month on a movie subscription service. That's $20 per month, which on the surface might not seem like that much.

However, that equates to $240 per year, which again might not seem like that big of a deal to make a fuss over. Remember though, you also have to consider the opportunity cost of this money.

You could instead invest that $240 into your retirement account and it could grow over the years to come. The same can't be said for spending your money on a music or movie service.

Once you spend that money, it's gone for good. I'm not saying that you have to cut all of your monthly expenses on things that aren't necessities, but you do need to become more aware of how bad it could be hurting you.

Your current income and the age when you plan on retiring will determine how many of these monthly expenses you need to cut back on. Start by taking an honest look at how often you actually use these different things.

For example, maybe you pay for cable and a movie/t.v. show subscription service. Determine which one it is that you use the majority of the time and cut the other one if you can.

Or maybe you only have cable, but you could save more money if you used a movie/t.v. show subscription service and stopped using cable. If you have cable, then you likely only watch a few of the channels you have access to anyways, so it might not be as hard to get rid of as you think.

If you're currently using a music subscription service, maybe you could consider listening to the radio. Yes, there would be some downsides to that because you wouldn't be able to play whatever you want whenever you want, but it'll save you money and that's the key.

The next monthly service I want you to think about is your cell phone. Yes, that's right your cell phone!

Take an honest look at how much you use it and what it is that you truly need it for. If you're on your phone constantly to check social media, then you really have to ask yourself if paying for data to check social media is worth it.

I want you to stop and think about what the purpose of a cell phone is. Its main use should be for communication right?

You need it to be able to call and text people. I'll also add that it's handy to be able to get on the internet and use a cell phone for GPS as well.

However, even with this being the case, we need to stop and ask ourselves if it's truly worth the cost. Having a cell phone plan that allows for unlimited data, text, and calls is expensive.

And if all of this data is being used to do things that could be done on your computer at home, then is it really worth it? I obviously can't answer that question for you, but cell phones are one of those things people pay so much for without ever realizing the true cost.

Not just with the cost of the monthly plan, but also in regards to the cell phone itself. Sometimes we get so caught up in what the monthly payment will be that we forget about the overall cost of the cell phone itself.

You can save a lot of money by getting a pay as you go phone. It likely won't be as bad as you think it is.

You can always adjust your minutes or data if you need to. Chances are good that you only regularly communicate with a few different people.

And I'm also willing to bet that a lot of text conversations you have aren't completely necessary. If you don't want to get a pay as you go phone, then consider cutting back on your plan if you can.

See how much data it is that you're using per month and look at how many texts you send, etc. Then pick a plan that' best for you. If you have kids, then don't be afraid to lay down the law.

Make it known that they're only allowed to use a certain amount of data per month or else there will be consequences. If they don't like this, then consider having them pay for their own bill if possible.

This will show them the true cost of a cell phone. Your kids don't have much room to complain if you cut back on your cell phone plan because you're the one paying for it in the first place.

Lastly, one other monthly expense that trips people up is a gym membership. Did you know that gyms actually expect that the majority of their members won't regularly come to the gym?

For example, if a gym expects to get 1,000 members based on the area it's in, the gym won't be built to accommodate that many members. Instead, it'll be built to suit a far less amount of people because the gym owners know that people aren't going to regularly show up.

This means that most people pay for a gym membership that they rarely use! Again it all comes down to being honest with yourself.

Do you currently have a gym membership and if so how often are you using it? If you regularly go, then great keep it.

However, if you don't go that often then consider canceling it. The truth is that you don't need a gym to be able to get a good workout in.

There are plenty of different ways that you can get an effective workout in at the comfort of your own home. For example, you could do bodyweight exercises at your home and the best part about that is that you wouldn't need any equipment.

You could also buy a set of resistance bands online for around $30 and you'll now have access to a whole host of exercises for a very cheap cost. Finally, if you have an extra room in your house or a shop, you could buy the equipment needed and have your own home gym.

With a gym membership, you're paying for a lot of stuff that you might not need. This all of course depends on what gym you go to because some of them are bare bones, while others have all of the amenities.

For example, you could be paying extra for a basketball court, swimming pool, and sauna, all of which you may or may not use. Instead, you can get the basics and set up your own gym.

You can get a pair of adjustable dumbbells and an adjustable bench to start with and build your way up from there. You really don't need as much equipment as you might think.

Paying up front for these things can save you a lot of money in the long run so don't be afraid to look into it. All in all though, when it comes to monthly expenses, you just need to take an honest look at how often it is that you really use these things and if it's worth the cost.

As an example, you might pay $10 a month for unlimited car washes. Normally one car wash at this place costs $7, so in your head you think it's worth it if you just go twice per month.

However, as times goes on you might realize that you rarely go to the car wash. Maybe you actually go on average once per month, which doesn't justify the cost. If that was the case, then you'd be paying more per car wash with the monthly service.

These companies aren't stupid. They wouldn't do something that would have them losing money.

They know the average amount of times that someone will go through the car wash for example. They'll then base the price and benefits of the service off of that knowledge.

The same thing goes for unlimited movies at the theater for only $10 per month. Most people won't see more than one movie per month, so at worst they'll break even with these people.

However, having this subscription service might entice people to go out and see a movie that they normally wouldn't because it's "free." Then once they're in the door, the hope is that they'll buy overpriced food and drinks at the concession stand.

This would of course be a sneaky way for the theater to increase revenue via the concession stand. Either way, if you do or don't go it's a win for the theater.

So in regards to monthly services always think of things from the business perspective and be honest with yourself about how often you'll use it.

That's the best way to not get sucked into these services that look like such a good deal on the surface.

Tip #5: Consider Transportation

The next big way you can save money is based on your transportation. Similar to a lot of the monthly charges seen above a lot of people buy cars without really thinking about different alternatives.

Having a car payment and everything that comes along with it seems to be an expense you just have to deal with. Of course, that isn't actually the case and thanks to modern technology and transportation you may have some nice alternatives.

Before we get into that though, let's first consider how expensive a car really is. The first and most obvious expense is the car itself. Someone might go out and buy a brand new car for $18,000 however the thing is that more than likely that person will have to take out a loan to be able to buy that car since he probably won't be able to pay for it upfront.

This loan will mean interest, which will mean that the cost of the car itself will cost more than $18,000. Then once you have the car, you'll have to regularly fill it up with gas.

You'll also have to take care of other maintenance things on the car such as oil changes and state inspections. We haven't even mentioned car insurance yet, which is another big expense to having a car.

Then of course, if anything goes wrong with the car, you're going to have to pay to get it fixed. If your car is still under warranty then great, if it's not however then you're likely going to be paying out of pocket to fix whatever is wrong with it.

These are expenses that no one really thinks about when it comes to owning a car. Finally, you also have to consider the fact that a car is considered to be a depreciating asset.

This means that it's value decreases over time. This makes sense because most car models are replaced by newer ones and the older cars will get more miles and wear and tear on them as time goes on.

But most people don't think about this decrease in value as losing money. In fact, it's estimated that a brand new car immediately loses 11% of its value as soon as you drive it off the lot, and up to 20% of its value within the first year.

This means that if you bought a new car for $20,000, its total value a year later could be as low as $16,000. Overall that adds up to one big expense when you think of the sum total of owning a car!

And what's the point of owning a car anyway? The point is to take you from one place to another!

As with a lot of the monthly expenses, the same rule of asking yourself "How much will I really use this and what do I need this for?", applies here. Ask yourself what is the purpose of you owning a car?

If you feel that it's the most efficient and effective way to take you from point A to point B, then great. However, if you want to get a car so you can show off to your coworkers, friends, and family, then maybe you should reconsider.

If you want to get a new car so you can have bluetooth speakers, a sunroof, or some other feature that isn't necessary for your given situation, then you should also reconsider. The rush of feelings of excitement and happiness from buying a new car will soon fade, but the car payment won't.

Now that we've covered how expensive buying a new car can be, let's look at some alternatives. The first one would be to get a used car or a car cheap enough to pay for upfront with cash.

Essentially when you do this, you're letting someone else take that initial depreciation hit when they drive it off the lot. If the used car is at least a year old, then it's already taken it's biggest depreciation hit.

Yes, the value will continue to decrease, but not by as large of a percentage per year as it did on the first year. Doing this can help save you a lot of money.

You're essentially passing up on the latest features that the newest model will carry but who cares about that? What's more important retiring early or driving a car with a cool gizmo?

Of course, you'll want to consider all of the factors such as if a warranty still exists on the used car you're interested in. If you're going to be driving a lot, then it may make sense to buy a new car if you feel there could be a lot of wear and tear due to the amount of driving you'd be doing.

Aside from buying a new car, you can also lease a car. There are two big downsides to leasing a car.

The first is that there are mile restrictions on how much you can drive the car. If you go over the amount, then you'll pay a big penalty.

The second and biggest downside is that you don't own the car. You'll keep making payments on it, but in the end, you won't own it.

In the case of buying your car, you can at least drive it around for as long as it'll last without making any more payments. You can also sell the car as well if you want to.

There might be specific situations where leasing a car makes sense though, maybe you're currently in a rural area, but are going to move to a city with better public transportation in a year or two.

If that's the case, you could lease a car for the time being and then be able to move on from it without having to take on any debt. The main point here is to consider your unique situation and look at all of the factors before making your decision.

The next option would be to use public transportation such as trains or buses. This is a great option to consider if you live in a city with good public transportation.

It's probably the cheapest means of transportation there is. Of course, it won't be able to take you to specific remote places, but it'll be able to get you to the major places you'd need to go.

You could also participate in a ridesharing service where essentially an app would connect you to a driver that can take you where you need to go. You of course don't have to use these two options independently of each other.

You can use public transportation whenever possible, and then when you need to go to specific places you can use the ridesharing service. Either way, using these methods of transportation will allow you to be able to cut out a lot of the expenses associated with owning a car such as gas, oil changes, maintenance repairs, state inspections, and insurance.

Finally, a bonus option you can consider is paying a friend or coworker to ride in his or her car. If the main place you need to be transported to is work, then this is a great option to consider.

This is especially true if your place of living isn't that far off from the route your coworker has to take to get to work. This may not be practical for everyone, but it's worth looking into.

Tip #6: Live Below Your Means

This next tip is a big one, and that's to live below your means. This is important for a lot of reasons, but it's especially important if you want to retire early.

The thing is though, that most people don't want to do this. And the reason for that is because it's hard!

Why live below your means when you have more money that you can spend on cool stuff? Stuff like bigger houses and fancier cars?

I mean how else are you supposed to let everyone know how much you make and signal to the world that you're an important person? This might seem silly, but this is what a lot of people will do.

They'll see what their monthly income is and then try to take on as big of a car payment and house payment as they can. Yes, we need shelter and a way to get from place to place, but there's a difference between necessary and excessive.

Some of the times when people are buying new houses or cars it's really in an effort to be able to show off more so than for practical reasons. You can certainly try to show off if you want to, just know that it'll cost you and it probably isn't worth it.

The first thing you have to ask yourself is why? Why do I want to live in the biggest house I can possibly afford?

Really be honest with yourself and see if it's because you're trying to impress other people. The reality is that most people could care less about what kind of house you live in!

If you don't believe me, then how often do you think or care about what kind of house other people live in? Hardly ever would be my guess.

You're likely more focused on what kind of house you live in. Not only is a larger house going to cost more per month, it could also tack on a higher interest payment if you're having to take out a larger loan to pay for the house in the first place.

Then you now have to furnish a larger house and maintain a larger house, which will undoubtedly have higher maintenance costs. You'll also be paying higher property taxes each year as well.

Finally and most importantly, it could cause you to miss out on your goal of early retirement. All because you wanted to live in a bigger house than you could actually afford.

I'm willing to bet though that you care more about retiring early than living in a big house. You'd rather have the freedom that comes about with retirement than to live in a big house that you can't even fully enjoy because you're always working to pay for the house.

Not only can living outside of your means cost you in your quest to retire early, but it can also strain you financially along the way. The reason for this is because you'll now be living paycheck to paycheck.

This'll make it harder for you to be able to save money each month, and if an emergency comes up, then it'll be a lot harder to pay for. All in all, it's not worth it to live above your means to look cool.

And this doesn't apply solely to houses and cars. It applies to plenty of other things such as designer shoes, clothes, accessories, and other items. Most of the time these items aren't any better than a cheaper version of the same thing.

What you're really paying for is the brand name. For example, a $10 pair of sunglasses that blocks UV rays isn't that much worse than a $100 pair that also blocks the same UV rays.

You likely want to buy the $100 pair because of a cool logo, hype marketing, or because your friend owns some. When it comes down to the practicality of them though, they aren't going to be much different.

Every purchase you make adds up, and it can add up to the difference between getting to retire early and having to keep working. Remembering this will help to keep things in perspective when you're making purchasing decisions.

At the end of the day, there are plenty of other little ways to save money. However, the tips listed above are the big things that you need to watch out for.

If you take care of those and are more conscious of what you spend your money on, then you should be good to go. Yes, you can do other things such as being more conservative with your water and electricity use, but you don't have to be a total penny pincher in order to retire early.

Not only that, but I'm sure you also want to be able to enjoy your retirement as well. It can be hard to do that if you're living in the dark in order to save money.

Chapter 6: How to Get Out of Debt Efficiently and Effectively

Now we're going to talk about how to get out of debt. Debt can be extremely crippling and it can prevent your dreams of early retirement from ever becoming a reality.

Sadly, there are certain expenses that most people feel like they just have to deal with. This could be something like a car or house payment. If you have a 30-year mortgage, then it can feel like it'll be forever before your house gets paid off.

Or maybe you're upside down in your car payment because your previous car wasn't paid off before you got a different car. It can feel impossible to get out of a situation like that as well.

Not only does the interest on these things eat you alive, but also the continual monthly payments. If you weren't in any debt, then you could start allocating this money towards something else.

And by something else, that would hopefully mean a retirement account of some kind. Therefore, it really is wise to be smart about when you're going to take on debt and what it is going to be used for.

Then you of course must be smart in how you're going to go about paying off that debt. If you take on debt for something that wasn't necessary or you go about paying off your debt inefficiently, then you're only holding yourself back. Let's first talk about when it's smart to take on debt and when it's not.

Is Debt Always a Bad Thing?

Some people think that taking on debt is always a bad thing. I can totally see why people think this.

Debt can have you living paycheck to paycheck, and the interest that occurs can be straining at times. However, the cool thing about debt is that it allows you to be able to buy things or get access to things that you normally wouldn't be able to.

It allows you to leverage other people's money so that you can get something you normally wouldn't be able to buy outright. The thing is though, you must be able to distinguish between good debt and bad debt.

There are some things that are probably going to be bad debt no matter how you look at it. For instance, if you take on some credit card debt because you want to go on a shopping spree, then that would be bad debt.

Sometimes the same purchase could be bad debt in one case and good debt in another case. An example of this could be a house.

Taking out a loan to buy a house can be a good thing since you need a place to live and the value of the house can go up over time. However, if you bite off more than you can chew by getting a house bigger than you can afford all of the sudden that loan could be considered bad debt not good.

The same thing goes for a car. If you decide buying a car is the most cost-effective way for your means of transportation, then that wouldn't necessarily be considered bad debt.

However, if you have to take out a larger loan so you can get the fancier model of the same car, then that's bad debt. You're either going to have a higher monthly payment, be paying on the car for a longer period of time, or have higher interest. There's no good way to slice it.

Another example of this could be taking out a loan to make an investment of some kind. If the investment pays off, then taking out a loan was a good move because it helped you make more money in the long run.

However, if you end up losing money on the deal, then it obviously wasn't worth it. The same could be said with going to college and student loans.

If you go to college and get an amazing high paying job thanks in part to your degree, then that loan you took out could be worth it. However, some people sadly get degrees that aren't as valuable in the marketplace and end up working low paying jobs that don't require a degree in the first place.

In these cases going to college isn't worth it. A lot of the time debt will be good or bad depending on the situation. Taking on debt to buy something usually means it's going to be a large purchase, so make sure that you really consider everything before you buy.

Taking out a loan is far easier than paying it off that's for sure. Regardless of whether or not you taking on debt was a good decision or a bad one, one thing still remains the same—you still need to pay back the money that you owe.

Even if you took out good debt, but go about paying it back in a bad way, then it will still hurt you. There are different viewpoints on the most efficient way to pay off debt. Let's cover them now.

How Should You Go About Paying Off Your Debt?

If you do have debt, then what's the best way that you should go about paying it off? While I don't believe that there's a one size fits all type of answer to this question, let's first start with what most people would agree is a terrible way to go about paying back your debts.

The worst way to go about paying off your debt is to pay the minimum on *all* of your debts. This holds true regardless of what the debt was for.

It doesn't matter if it's a car, house, or credit card payment. Paying the minimum on any of these things will only haunt you later on.

Let's take buying a car for example. Most of the time when people buy a car, they only focus on what the monthly payment will be. They don't focus on the interest rate, how long the duration of the loan will be, or the overall final price that they'll be paying for the car.

And the thing is that car dealers know this. That's why they'll manipulate the numbers however they can in order to get you the monthly payment that you want.

They know the main thing that matters is the final overall price you pay for the car. That's what they focus on and they have good reason to do so.

From now on, I want you to do the same. Consider different interest rates you'll have to pay based on how large or small your monthly payment will be.

Paying the minimum will cause you to pay more interest over time. And the more interest you pay, the less you'll have left to put towards other things.

It all comes back to opportunity cost. One argument you could make for paying the minimum is that you could use the leftover capital to invest in other things.

This could pay off if what you make off of those other investments is higher than what the interest rate is on whatever loans you have. However, in the majority of cases, the interest rates will typically be higher.

The safer bet is to pay more than the minimum. With that being said though, how much should you pay? And in what order should you pay off your debts?

This is where there are some different schools of thought. The first way some recommend to go about paying off your debts is to pay the minimum on all of your loans except for the highest interest one.

You'll then put all of your efforts and focus into paying off that highest interest loan. Once that loan is taken care of, you'll then move onto the next highest interest loan and focus solely on paying that debt off while still paying the minimum on everything else.

You'll use the money you were paying on the first loan to help you pay off the next one. You'll keep on repeating this process until everything is paid off.

For example, let's say you have 5 different loans. The highest interest debt you have is a credit card with 17% interest and the total debt on that card is $1,500.

Let's say the minimum monthly payment on that card is $50, but you decide you can pay $300 per month on it to get rid of it as soon as possible. In the meantime, while this credit card is getting paid off, you'll be paying the minimum on everything else.

Then once that credit card is paid off, you'll then put that $300 and any extra money you have towards paying off the next highest interest rate loan. Once that loan is paid off, you'll take all of the money you were paying on it and put it towards the next debt and so on and so forth until all 5 of these debts are paid off.

This is the best way to go about paying off your debt if you want to save some money on interest. However, what this method doesn't take into consideration is human psychology.

If you're someone who doesn't get swayed from the plan easily and can stick to something without seeing the payoff for a while, then this would be a great method for you to try.

On the other hand, if you like to build momentum and get small wins along the way, then I would say that the other method is better for you. What it really comes down to is what you'll be able to stick to.

Not what's logically supposed to be the best or what your neighbor is doing to pay off his debt. Know yourself and base your plan of action to pay off your debt based on that.

It doesn't matter if the first method I shared will allow you to save on interest in the long run if you're not able to stick to the plan. If you're not able to stick with it, then you won't pay off your debt and you'll pay more interest in the long run anyway.

The other method of paying off your debt involves paying off your smallest debt first. Rather than focusing on the debt with the highest interest, you'll instead focus on which balance is the lowest overall.

To pay it off you'll pay the minimum on everything else, and then put any extra money towards paying off that balance. Then once that balance is paid off, you'll put all of the money you were paying on that loan plus anything else you can towards the next lowest balance loan.

Once that loan is paid off, you'll then take all of that money and use it to pay off the next lowest balance and so on and so forth. Like I just mentioned this is a great method to consider doing because it takes into account human motivation.

It's exciting and relieving to see a loan completely gone and not have to worry about it anymore. That's why I prefer this way of going about paying off your debts to the other method for most people.

Of course, these aren't the only ways that you can go about paying back your debt. You can also try to pay off your old credit cards with lower interest credit cards.

This strategy can allow you to pay less interest over time and give you more time to pay off your balance. It may not be practical or even possible to do this though depending on what your credit score is, but it's worth considering.

All in all, when it comes to getting out of debt, it really comes down to being smart with the money that you have and allocating every dollar you can towards getting out of debt. And of course, remember to not spend more than you make. It's often the simplest tips that get overlooked.

Chapter 7: Tips to Help Improve Your Credit Score

Now let's talk about some tips to help you improve your credit score. In case you're unfamiliar, your credit score is a number used to evaluate the likeliness that you'll pay back your debts.

The higher your score is the better. People have different standards for what's considered good and what's bad, but in general, a score of 700 or higher is generally considered to be good.

Having a higher credit score will make it easier for you to be able to get loans on big purchases that you'll make throughout your life such as a house or car. A better credit score will also allow you to be able to get lower interest rates on these purchases, which will allow you to save a lot of money over the long haul.

Since the main goal is early retirement here, you're obviously going to want to save as much money as you possibly can, which is why improving your credit score matters.

Credit Score Myths

Before we get into how to actually improve your credit score, let's first talk about some common myths in regards to credit score. There are a lot of myths out there when it comes to credit score, however I'm only going to share with you the myths that I believe to be the most harmful.

The first one is that you should leave a balance on your credit card. The idea is that doing this will help you to improve your credit score.

Not only will this not help you improve your credit score, but it'll hurt you. If you leave a balance on your credit card, then you'll have to pay interest on that balance and that's something that we want to avoid.

When it comes to paying your credit card, the ideal situation is to wait until the end of the month when you get the bill and then pay all of it off so that you don't have a remaining balance. This would be better than using your credit card and immediately paying it because that could show up as you always having a zero balance, which might make it look like you're not even using the credit card.

The next common myth is that checking your credit score will hurt your score. This is one that I believed for most of my adult life, and I'm sure that you've heard of it too.

If you don't know what your credit score is, then it can be hard to know if it needs to be improved or if you should keep doing what you're doing. Imagine if our health got hurt every time we tried to check our blood pressure.

It would sure make things harder to know if we need to improve or not! Thankfully though, if you check your credit score online using credit scoring services, then you shouldn't have to worry about taking a hit on your credit score.

It's only when a place such a bank checks your score that it can hurt you. These are known as hard pulls on your credit score because the institution that is considering lending you money is looking at your credit history.

When you go online and check your credit score using a credit scoring service, this is known as a soft pull and you don't have to worry about taking a hit on your credit with soft pulls.

Another common myth is that it can be hard to ruin a good credit score. The truth is that it can only take a few short months to ruin years of hard work to build up your score.

Letting an account sit unpaid for too long can result in something known as a charge-off. This is when a creditor no longer tries to collect after a certain period of delinquency.

A single instance such as having one charge-off can greatly affect your overall score. If you think about it, this isn't just true for your credit score, but most things in life.

You could build a friendship over years and years and then have it ruined over a single argument. Athletes can work their way up to a certain level of conditioning over years of hard training only to lose most of it in a few short months.

The point here is to stay on top of your game at all times when it comes to your credit score. If you have a good credit score, then don't deviate from what it was that got you that good score to begin with.

Conversely, another common credit score myth is that you're not able to improve a bad credit score. Yes, it may seem daunting to try and take a credit score in the low 500s into the 700s, but it is possible.

The problem with this myth is that if you don't believe it's possible to improve your credit score, then you won't do anything about it. You'll keep on making the same mistakes and falling back into old habits, which will of course keep your credit score low.

And as with most things in life, when you find yourself in a deep hole, it can take a while to get out of it. Take losing weight for example.

If someone steadily gained weight over the years, it can take that person some time to lose the weight. It won't happen overnight, and the situation also won't get any better if the person doesn't believe that change is possible.

These last two myths deal with debt and the first one is that you need to take on a large amount of debt in order to improve your credit score. The truth is that you don't need to take on a large amount of unnecessary debt in order to improve your credit score.

Doing that doesn't make much sense in the grand scheme of things if you think about it. The point of a credit score is to be able to get a loan and have a good interest rate.

The reason why you want a good interest rate is that you can save money over the long run. However, if you take on more debt than you need to, you're only spending more money that you don't even have to begin with!

It's almost as if you're spending more money now to hopefully save some money on a future loan. You don't need to get so caught up in trying to improve your credit score that you make unwise financial decisions.

Doing something as simple as using your credit card for gas and groceries and paying the bill at the end of the month can be enough to get a good credit history started.

The final myth that I'm going to talk about here in this book is kind of like an opposite to the previous one and that is the belief that you should never take on any debt.

Like I mentioned in the previous chapter, there's good debt and bad debt. It all depends on what you're taking a loan out for. And also just because you aren't in debt, that doesn't mean that your credit score is good.

You could've been in bad debt for years and just gotten out of it. It could take a while to get your credit score back on track.

Also if you're debt free because you declared bankruptcy, then that doesn't mean that your credit score is good either.

How to Improve Your Credit Score

Now that you're aware of some common credit score myths out there, let's now dive into how you can actually go about improving your credit score. The first thing that you must do when it comes to improving your credit score is to not be afraid to face reality.

You can't be afraid to know the truth of how bad your current credit score situation is. Most people who are afraid their score is bad live in denial and refuse to check their score because they don't want to see something that they won't like.

If you're afraid to check your credit score because you fear it may be bad don't worry it's not your fault. Growing up we don't learn anything about credit scores in school and we likely learned what we know about credit cards from our parents.

That could be a good or a bad thing depending on who raised you. Regardless it is still your responsibility to take matters into your own hands to take your current credit score and improve upon it.

That can of course seem like a scary thing to do, but credit doesn't have to be a scary topic if you arm yourself with the proper knowledge.

Not checking your credit score creates an obvious problem and that is the fact that it's hard to improve on something if you don't know what the numbers are. Imagine if you were trying to increase the amount of money you had in your checking account but you're not able to check the amount of money that's in that account.

How would you ever know if you're getting better or not? You wouldn't and the same thing can be said for your credit score.

You must first start by checking your credit score with a soft pull so that it won't affect your score. Then once you know that number, you'll know what the health of your credit score is.

It's kind of like taking your blood pressure. Once the reading pops up, you'll know if it's good or bad.

If the number is good, then great, keep on doing what you're doing. On the other hand, if it's bad, then you know that you need to change some things.

Most of the time when it comes to credit scores, it shouldn't be too hard to find out what's causing the problem just like with the bad blood pressure reading. For example, if you're blood pressure reading was bad and you know that you eat fast food every night for dinner, then that's probably something you need to stop doing.

Similarly, if you've had unpaid balances for years on end, then that's probably a good place to start.

The second and most obvious tip is to pay your bill on time. Making late payments or having to settle can be a red flag that you don't pay back the money that you owe on time.

It's also important to note that if you have a leftover balance on any of your cards paying that off can help your credit score out as well. Of course, this isn't to say that you should neglect your current monthly credit card bill in favor of paying off an old balance.

Most of the damage has probably already been done if that old balance hasn't been paid off. Late payments from years ago have less of an impact on your credit score than current late payments.

And if you think about it, that makes sense. Your credit score is always updating and being adjusted based on how likely it is you can pay back money in the present day.

An overall history of years and years should be able to give any potential lenders a good track record to look at. However, if you were late on a payment 3 years ago and have been good ever since, that late payment should have less of an impact on your score than if you were to miss a payment last week.

The next tip is the keep your credit utilization ratio in check. Your credit utilization ratio is the ratio between your total credit limit and how much of that limit you use.

For example, let's say you have a credit limit of $7,000. During that month you go out and spend $6,500 on that card.

That would be a credit utilization ratio of 93%, which looks really bad. This means that in one month, you used 93 percent of the available limit on your card.

The reason why this is bad on your credit score is that acting in this behavior makes it look as if you're in a bad financial situation or you're financially desperate. It could also be a sign of more reckless behavior in the future such as taking out more credit cards and getting close to maxing them out.

Most agree that not letting your ratio go above 30% is good. In this case with a limit of $7,000, this would mean not going above $2,100.

This is also why it may be a good idea to leave an old credit card account open even if you don't plan on using it. This will allow your overall credit limit to be higher and thus you'll have more wiggle room in regards to your credit utilization ratio.

Of course, you really have to know yourself. If you know that leaving that credit card open is just going to cause you to use it later on and spend more money that you don't have, then it probably is for the best that you go ahead and close it.

Focusing on these two tips of not going above 30% on your credit utilization and paying your bill on time account for over half the battle to improving your credit score. It really is that simple and it doesn't have to be complicated.

Often times the simplest solution is the best one, however that doesn't mean that simple is easy. In regards to improving your health, everyone knows that you need to eat better foods and exercise, that's simple.

Actually doing it though is where people trip up. And the same thing goes for our credit scores.

It's not too hard to figure out that paying your credit card bills on time will help out your credit score, however doing that each and every month can be hard at times because life happens. The toilet in your house stops working or your car needs repairs.

These things pop up and we can't predict when they're going to happen. That's why the next tip to helping improve your credit score is to be prepared.

We know that life is crazy and random financial emergencies are going to jump up out of nowhere and try to surprise us. With that being the case, why not go ahead and be prepared for emergencies.

Start saving money and cutting back on other expenses to help prepare yourself for the storm that you know will be coming. This way when a big expense does come, you'll be prepared and able to handle it.

That's far better than not having the money available so you use a credit card, and then when the bill comes you have no way of paying it back so you let it sit there and start to occur late fees.

And now you have no way of paying those fees so you continue to let it sit there and occur more fees and so on and so forth until you're in thousands of dollars of debt and your credit score is shot.

If you have the money saved up, then you're in control. You can more easily allow your credit utilization ratio to stay below 30%, and you can use your credit card without worry because you know you have the money to pay it off when the bill comes at the end of the month.

To continue with our health analogy, who do you think is more likely to eat healthily, the person who's already prepared a healthy meal and stored it in a container in his refrigerator for when he gets home or the person who comes home with nothing prepared and junk food in the refrigerator?

It's obvious that the person with a healthy meal already cooked and prepared is way more likely to eat healthy because he set himself up for success. The other person is probably tired after a long day at work and he might not feel like cooking.

So he'll just drive through a fast food restaurant and eat a burger and fries for dinner. All in all, if you're able to stay prepared, pay your bills on time, and keep your utilization ratio below 30%, then you'll be able to increase your credit score over time and keep it high.

Yes, it could take a while, but you might as well start making these changes now. It won't do you any good to continue falling back into old habits.

With that being said, there is something else you can try that might work faster for you to be able to increase your credit score. This tactic is something known as piggybacking.

Essentially what you'll do is get signed on as an authorized user for someone else's credit card. Obviously, it'll be someone that trusts you, be it a close friend, family member, coworker, or someone along those lines.

And that person won't have to worry about your credit history showing up on their report. Only the primary cardholder's history will show up on the authorized user's history.

And the authorized user can also be removed from the account at any time. This is different from cosigning, and in that case, the cosigner would not be able to be removed from the card until the account is paid in full and closed.

Once you're signed on as an authorized user for that card, you'll receive all of the credit history for that card as long as it's reported to the credit bureaus. This is an important first step that you'll want to make sure that you take.

If this credit card isn't going to report you as an authorized user to the credit bureaus, then it does you no good to be an authorized user on the account. Signing on as an authorized user can be a great thing if the person you're signing on with has a long and good history of using credit cards.

Doing this could help increase your credit score rather quickly. Of course, you'll want to make sure that you're signing on with someone who has good credit and not bad credit and you also want to check what their credit utilization ratio is as well.

If their credit utilization is above 30%, then that can still negatively impact their score even if the person is paying his or her bills on time. It's also important to note that even if you use this strategy to try and get a loan it may not help you out.

For example, let's say you use this method to try and increase your credit score to help you get a loan for an automobile. When they do a hard pull on your credit they might notice that all of your accounts are as an authorized user and deny you even though your score is good.

Ultimately this strategy may or may not work, but it's worth a shot if you've got nothing else to lose. The best thing you can do in regards to your credit score is to be responsible with your accounts over a long period of time, which you shouldn't have trouble doing if your main focus is to retire early!

Conclusion

You now have everything you need in order to start down the path to successfully retire early. All that's left for you to do is execute on the plan. Of course, that's easier said than done, but you'll be glad that you did.

You have to stay focused on controlling your finances now or else they'll control you for the rest of your life. You need to keep early retirement in mind with every financial decision it is that you're going to make.

Doing so will help you to stay focused on the end goal. Money is something that everyone has to deal with, yet most people try to ignore their money problems as much as they can.

They're in crippling debt and their retirement situation isn't that good, yet they continue to make poor financial decisions. Like I just said, if you don't control your money, then it'll control you.

Your money will find somewhere else to go if you don't know what to do with it. We're constantly bombarded with ads, businesses, and other people telling us how we should spend our money. And if we don't know how to use it wisely, then it can be easy to fall into the trap of being a consumer looking for the next latest and greatest thing to buy.

Instead of being like most people, do the opposite. Start by taking a hard look at your current financial situation. It may not be pretty, but it's better to face the truth now rather than to have to face it later on down the line when it may be too late to turn things around.

This is the very first step you have to take if you want things to change. By doing this, you'll be able to see what the problem is and then you can come up with a game plan in order to fix it.

Don't be afraid to look at everything. Look at your retirement account. Look at how much debt you're currently in, what your income is right now, and how much money you have saved up.

Maybe you'll find out that being in a lot of debt is what's holding you back. You could be paying too high of interest rates on your current loans and the monthly payments could be too high.

You could consider refinancing certain loans or focus all of your attention on paying off the debts. Then once you do, you can start pouring all of that extra money into your retirement account.

However, none of this will be able to happen if you're not willing to face reality, which might be tough depending on what your situation is. After taking a look at things, you want to set a goal for when it is that you want to retire by.

Imagine being an archer without a target to aim for. That is what it's going to be like if you don't set a target date for when you'd like to retire by.

If you want to set a more ambitious retirement goal, that's completely fine as long as you're willing to make the necessary sacrifices. If you want to retire sooner rather than later you could be living significantly below your means in order to pull that off.

And that's great if that's what you want to do, just know what the price of early retirement is and be willing to pay that price.

Once you've taken that step, you then need to figure out what to do next so that you can make your goal a reality. This will mean different things for different people.

You might not be in any debt, but you might spend all of your money frivolously, in which case you need to figure out how you can start saving more money. Maybe it's your car payment that's holding you back and you need to pay it off as soon as possible so that you can get back on the right track.

Or maybe your current problem is that you don't make enough money right now so you need to do some things on the side apart from your main source of income to bring in some extra money.

Whatever the biggest glaring problem is in regard to your current financial situation, figure it out, and then try to tackle it head-on with everything you can. This, of course, doesn't mean that you should neglect other aspects of your financial health, but you definitely want to tackle the thing that's holding you back the most first.

From there all you really need to do is stay the course and you'll reach your goal. For example, let's say your car payment is what you determine to be holding you back the most.

Your car payment is $350 per month and once that extra money is freed up you could put that much more into your retirement account. You would focus your attention on the car by putting any extra money you could towards paying off the car.

In the meantime, while the car is being paid off, you would still pay all of your other bills, put some money into your retirement account, and save some money each month. The reason for this is because you don't want an emergency to come up and have to pay for it with credit cards.

That will cause you to incur more interest and that'll be another uphill battle that you have to fight. Then once your car is paid off or any other debts you have for that matter, you can really go full force and put as much money as possible per month into your retirement account.

All you have to do from this point is stay the course, as long as you're making good contributions to your retirement account and you're aware of what you're spending your money on, you should be well on your way to early retirement.

Never lose sight of the goal and don't be afraid to live below your means in order to hit your target retirement date. The main thing that you want to achieve is early retirement, not living in a big fancy house or driving a luxury car.

Most people aren't willing to live below their means. They want to show the world how important they are with a flashy car and fancy house.

The thing that makes retirement so hard for most people is that it's years and years away. You have to delay gratification for many years before you see the rewards from all of the sacrifices that you've made.

It's much easier to instead seek instant gratification. If you want the brand new big screen T.V. today, then go ahead and get it using a credit card.

You can get it now and worry about how you're going to pay for it later. It's obvious to see that engaging in those kinds of behaviors is the easy thing to do.

However, decisions like these are what come back to haunt you later on. Think of how crushing it would be for someone to want to retire but have to keep on working past the normal age of retirement all because of poor decisions that person made with his or her money throughout his or her life?

I don't want you to have to go through that same feeling of regret because it'll be too late to change anything at that point. Instead, do what you have to now in order to reap the benefits later on.

You'll be so glad that you did. Then once you're retired, you'll literally have the freedom to do what it is that you want.

That's probably why it is that you want to retire in the first place. You want to have the freedom from your job.

You might be sick and tired of having to be at the same place Monday-Friday 9-5. You might be sick and tired of having to ask off to go on vacation or to go to a doctor's appointment.

You might want to travel more, or you might want to have more time to spend with your friends and family. Or maybe you just want to play golf or watch T.V. on a Wednesday afternoon.

Retirement will allow you to be able to do these things and early retirement will allow you to take advantage of this even sooner than most people even dream of. When you're starting to lose motivation, remember the reason why it is that you're doing this in the first place and that can help keep you going.

And the cool part is that if you did things right, then you shouldn't have to worry about running out of money. You embraced whatever money problems you had and tackled them head on so that you wouldn't have to worry about it later on.

You put in the hard work upfront of earning the money in the first place, but then you were also wise with how you used it. If you make every dollar you have count, then you can run circles around people who make way more money than you but decide to spend it foolishly.

This journey will not be fast and easy, but it will take years of patience and dedication depending on where you're starting point is. Even with that being the case, I encourage you to keep the flame of early retirement burning bight and never let the flame completely wither.

If you do that, then you won't have any chance of achieving the goal. I know it's within you to be able to pull this off, so stay strong and stick to the plan and you'll get there!

Did you enjoy reading this book? If so, please consider leaving a review. Even just a few words would help others decide if the book is right for them. Best regards and many thanks in advance—Andrew.

Sources

(1)https://www.cnbc.com/2017/08/24/most-americans-live-paycheck-to-paycheck.html

(2)https://www.gobankingrates.com/retirement/planning/why-americans-will-retire-broke/

(3)https://www.cleveland.com/business/index.ssf/2016/01/why_do_70_percent_of_lottery_w.html

(4)https://www.theguardian.com/law/2011/apr/11/judges-lenient-break

www.ingramcontent.com/pod-product-compliance
Lightning Source LLC
Chambersburg PA
CBHW020550220526
45463CB00006B/2252